T0064297

MISERABLE

BUT

MOTIVATED

How the Names of God Motivate
Worship in Miserable Circumstances

BEN HAMMOND

WESTBOW·
PRESS
A DIVISION OF THOMAS NELSON
& ZONDERVAN

WestBow Press books may be ordered through booksellers or by contacting:

WestBow Press
A Division of Thomas Nelson & Zondervan
1663 Liberty Drive
Bloomington, IN 47403
www.westbowpress.com
1 (866) 928-1240

ISBN: 978-1-4908-8626-8 (sc)
ISBN: 978-1-4908-8628-2 (hc)
ISBN: 978-1-4908-8627-5 (e)

Library of Congress Control Number: 2015909945

Print information available on the last page.

WestBow Press rev. date: 7/24/2015

To my wife Lori, who believed that I could write this book and encouraged me to do it. I love you!

Contents

Introduction

Do you always *feel* like worshiping God? If you are discussing this book in a small group study, go ahead and say "yes." I don't want you to publicly brand yourself as a sinner before you even get started. In your heart, though, consider the question at a deeper level. Do you *really* feel like worshiping God? Chances are, sometimes your emotions are flat. You've asked God for something and He has not delivered. You have been diagnosed with a chronic or terminal disease. Your prayers seem to dissipate into oblivion once they clear the roof of your house. How can you praise God when things are so bad? Does He even deserve your worship?

Sure, we find it easy to offer up praise when He pours blessings on us. In church we stand up and testify about what He has done for us in the past week. On Thanksgiving Day we take a more detailed inventory of everything we appreciate in our lives. However, what about those times that the miserable circumstances He has allowed us to endure overshadow the blessings?

I have good news for you. He deserves our worship anyway. The worthiness of God does not depend on what He is doing for us. It depends on who He is. His character qualifies Him to receive our worship.

If we really want to learn how to worship God, we have to

know who He is. One of the best ways to learn about Him is to study His names, as it is through His names that He has revealed certain aspects of His character.

As we embark on this adventure, we will study fourteen names of God. Some of these may be familiar to you, while others may be new. As an added bonus, I will also throw in the names of two altars and a city, as these provide important information that we need to know about God's character.

By the time we reach the end of this book, it is my prayer that we will have learned enough about God to be motivated to worship Him even when He allows us to be miserable. I invite you to come along with me on this journey as we discover how to worship our great God, even when we don't feel like it!

Ben Hammond

Chapter 1

The *Worthiness* of His Name

Bless the LORD, O my soul: and all that is within me, bless his holy name!
(Psalm 103:1 NKJV)

Why can't I be like that? I wonder how many times those words cross my mind as I peruse flowery books penned by authors who present themselves as saintly supermen. Every spiritual discipline in which they engage provides feelings of pure ecstasy. Each morning they wake up with a song on their lips, audibly praising God for a beautiful new day. Although they admit to some struggles along the way, the difficulties pale in insignificance when compared with the inner delight they find in constant fellowship with God. They are, for all practical purposes, perfect.

Then there are the rest of us. When the alarm clock mercilessly wrenches us out of a blissful coma in the morning, we come perilously close to heaving it across the room. Any brave soul who dares offer a "good morning" immediately gets etched into the black list for the remainder of the day. More often than not, when we sit down to read the Bible, our minds begin to wander. When we glance into the mirror, no holy glow frames our reflection. It's just not fair. Why do some folks get all the joy that causes them

1

to break out into spontaneous praise to God while the rest of us are bogged down with the difficulties of life?

If the truth were known, I think most of us would fall into the second category. Sometimes we feel excitement about God, and it seems natural to offer up praises. Other times, however, the feelings go AWOL. It may be that God dared to do something that did not meet our approval. Or it could be that we're just having a bad day. Occasionally our circumstances in life may cause us to feel downright miserable. It is against our nature to praise God when we feel this way. So what are we to do?

Here is the answer: praise Him anyway. Sounds simple, doesn't it? If you think so, give it a try. Next time you are tempted to crawl under a rock and disappear, try to hum a happy little tune. It doesn't matter which one. Try one you learned in Sunday school or church. Hum a few bars of "Jesus Loves Me." If you really can't ratchet up any spirituality, go for Barney's theme song or the latest country hit. Just sing *something*. Not easy, is it?

David, the celebrated king of Israel, knew what it was like to have trouble. He also knew what to do about it. To his own soul (yes, he was talking to himself), he exclaimed, "Bless the Lord . . . bless His holy name!" (Psalm 103:1). Did he always feel like worshiping God? Probably not. Fortunately, we do not have to *feel* anything to worship. However, we do have to *know* something. We have to know who God is and what He is like. He deserves worship when He opens the windows of heaven and lavishes gifts on us, but He also deserves worship when He seems distant and uncaring. It is His character, rather than the favors that He bestows on us, that makes Him worthy of worship.

If God wants us to worship Him based on His character, it stands to reason that He would describe Himself to us. One of the ways He accomplishes this is by revealing names that illustrate certain aspects of His character. If we understand His names, we understand Him.

Have you ever considered what life would be like if we did not have names? That sounds silly, I know. But humor me for a moment and consider how difficult life would be. Without names, we would be forced refer to each other by some vague, descriptive term. We would quickly tire of calling everyone "Hey, you!" Some of the sanctity of my wedding day would have been lost if in making vows to my love, I would have gazed into her eyes and pronounced, "I, twenty-five-year-old man with dark hair, take you, light-haired woman, to be my lawfully wedded wife . . ." It just loses some of the intimacy, wouldn't you agree?

Names are intrinsically bound to a person. At the mere mention of a name, a massive database of information comes flooding to our minds. For example, if I should mention George Washington, most likely your mind would immediately conjure up an image of a man sporting a hideous wig, bravely crossing the icy Delaware River through a thick blanket of fog. Your mind would also wander to the bloody American Revolution, and you may even contemplate the greatness of the United States that we know and love today. All this because of the simple mention of two seemingly innocuous words. These words, however, describe a man and all that he represents.

Unfortunately, names are not quite as meaningful to us today as they were in biblical times. I am not suggesting that we are careless about choosing names for our children. When my wife was pregnant with each of our four children, we pored over books and websites that listed names we had never heard of before, including some we would not give to our children if it were the last name on Earth. Sure, we gave halfhearted thought to the meaning of the names, but there were more important issues at stake. For example, how would this particular moniker jibe with our last name? Did anyone else in the family have that name? My oldest son and my daughter were given the respective middle names of James and Nichole. These are the only ones that we had predetermined to use, as they are the middle names of my wife and me. We also considered such vital questions as whether or not I knew anyone in my childhood with a certain name. If that kid from third grade sparked bad memories in my mind, his name was scratched from the list. I refused to name my children anything that reminded me of bullies or runny noses. My wife began to worry that we might have to settle for an obscure biblical name such as Mahershalalhashbaz or Samgarnebo (see Isaiah 8:1 and Jeremiah 39:3 if you think I made them up).

Your parents probably experienced a similar turmoil that caused them to teeter on the edge of marital disharmony while coming up with something to call you. Your name was likely born out of great suffering, and therefore it is something you should wear with pride. It refers to you. It is personal. Although someone else may share your name, it is still yours. And pity the person who gets it wrong.

Does it disgust you when someone mispronounces your name? One of my biggest pet peeves is when someone spells my last name as "Hammonds." I always patiently explain that there is only one of me. I am a "Hammond" and not a "Hammonds." This also extends to the name of the town in which one lives. How you pronounce Louisville or Lafayette is not a matter of opinion, but a hard and fast rule that is jealously protected by speakers of the local dialect. The innocent tourist who inadvertently gets it wrong quickly discovers that some residents "born and bred" in these towns possess a rather strong loyalty to the pronunciation of their native land.

Do you know what your name means? My name, Benjamin, hails from the Hebrew language. In the Bible, Jacob's twelfth son was originally named Benoni, which means "son of my sorrow."[1] He received this name from his mother, Rachel, just before she died in childbirth. His father, however, apparently did not wish to be continuously faced with the depressing memory of the death of his favorite wife. He renamed the latest addition to his family "Benjamin," which means "son of the right hand,"[2] indicating a favored child who would prove to be a blessing to his parents. I am not sure if my parents believed in my potential to become a blessing to them when I was nothing more than a wrinkled newborn screaming from the bassinet, but I am proud of my name. I hope that it aptly describes what I have become.

God also has a name that describes who He is. Actually, He has several. Through the course of biblical history, He revealed these names one at a time to His people, allowing them to discover something new and exciting about His character. Sometimes He did this when He was about to charge them with a big task, and sometimes when He was imparting a stern warning of coming punishment. In these times, He did not delve into an extended dissertation about who He was or what He was going to do. He simply revealed a previously unknown name, and the name would say it all.

Studying the names of God, therefore, is much more than a mere intellectual pursuit. God progressively revealed His names to His people because they needed to know something about Him that would influence their actions in a specific situation. The more they knew about His character, the better they could serve Him. As we serve the same God revealed in the Bible, a study of His names provides us also with applications for how we should function in our daily lives. Furthermore, the truths we discover about Him through His names give us undeniable reason to worship Him.

In the Bible we find many commands to worship God. However, this often proves to be more difficult than it appears.

It seems that few people can agree on the finer points of worship. Does it require professional singers, musical instruments, dimmed rooms, or flashing lights? Are we supposed to sit silently in our pews with our heads bowed, or should we stand in the aisle with our hands lifted toward the rafters?

People engage in the experience of worship in many different ways. Some folks are naturally expressive, while others have more reserved personalities. I have been in churches where everyone prays out loud simultaneously. In other assemblies, I have feared that if someone ventured an audible "amen," four or five folks would doubtless have a stroke. In some services you have to fight off sleep during the singing, while in others earplugs would be in order. We are all unique, so I cannot tell you exactly what forms of worship you should use. What I want to do instead is to lay the foundation for worship. Rather than discussing *how* we should worship, let's take a look at *why* we should worship.

The answer can be found in the names of God. As we study His revealed names, we should keep in mind that we are not to worship Him just for what He does for us, but for who He is. He deserves worship because of His nature.

Most of us, at some point in our lives, find ourselves in the desert as far as our worship of God is concerned. The passion dissipates, and the previously brilliant flame seems to have dwindled to barely a spark. What has happened? Has the worthiness of God changed? Has He somehow lost the glory that we once perceived in Him? Donald Whitney reminds us in this case that "when worship becomes empty, the problem lies with the subject (us), not the object (God)."[3] He is *always* worthy of our worship. As we study the names of God, we will develop a better understanding of His nature and character. It is my prayer that our deeper appreciation of His character will instill, as Bill Thrasher puts it, "an inner delight in our hearts to do His will."[4]

Before we jump into our discussion of the specific names of God, however, we need to set the foundation. The foundation is that He is holy. That alone makes Him worthy of worship.

God's Name is Holy

In Jesus' model prayer, commonly known as the Lord's Prayer, recognition of God's name takes priority. Jesus opened this prayer with "Our Father in heaven, hallowed be Your name" (Matthew 6:9). The word "hallowed" is an Old English word that describes the process of making something holy or consecrating it for a particular use. Of course, we can do nothing to make God's name holy. His name is holy because He is holy. Our responsibility is to recognize His holiness and honor His name above everything else in our lives.

Before we begin our investigation into the names of God, we need to stop and ask ourselves whether or not we honor His name appropriately. Maybe you like to pray the Lord's Prayer verbatim. Perhaps you prefer to use it as a model. But does His name occupy the place of highest prominence in your life?

Back in my high school days, a friend and I installed some old citizen band (CB) radios in our vehicles. As we ventured into this new hobby, we quickly realized that every serious CB user possessed a unique handle. A handle was a pseudonym that allowed communication without revealing actual names. You could develop an on-the-road relationship with an unseen truck driver known as "Papa Bear" or "Boss Man" and never know what he looked like or which section of the country he called home. The impersonal nature of CB communication discouraged requests for a person's real name. As we examine the names of God, we will begin to recognize that they act as much more than simple handles that give us something to call our Creator. Rather, they serve as portraits of some aspect of His character.

If God's names relate closely to His character, we must ask a very important question. How do we treat these names? A vast amount of disrespect for everything sacred has crept into our society, most notably with respect to God. I always cringe when I hear someone use the name of God carelessly. We could learn a lesson from the Jews who meticulously ensure that they honor God's name. In fact, even in English we often find His name spelled "G-d" in Jewish writings. They make it a point to be sure that they never deface the name of God. We can trace the history behind this tradition to the time that God ordered the Israelites to destroy everything that pertained to the false gods of the Canaanites. The instructions included the command to "destroy their names from that place" (Deuteronomy 12:3). The name of their own God, however, must be treated with care. In the next verse God instructed them to "not do so unto the LORD your God" (KJV). Many Jews interpret this as a broad prohibition against treating their God in the same manner as they were to treat the false gods, thus defacing the name of Jehovah.[5] They take this command so seriously that they believe that if one were to write the name of God on a piece of paper, and that paper was erased or handled irreverently, it would bring disrespect to the name of God. Therefore, refusing to write out the name of God provides a buffer that prohibits the inadvertent mishandling God's holy name.

The debate over the handling of God's written name extends even into the digital world. The proliferation of technology has raised questions that Jews of former generations never would have imagined. For example, is it acceptable to type God's name into a computer? After all, turning off the screen would erase the name of God. Furthermore, a computer screen constantly refreshes itself faster than the eye can see. Does that bring dishonor to God's name? Rabbi Mordecai Friedman attempts to answer this question, explaining his belief that typing God's name into a computer is acceptable because it never truly exists physically, being simply a combination of temporary energized pixels.[6] When printed out, however, the hardcopy becomes permanent. If God's name appeared on the printout, it could never be destroyed. For that reason, some Jews still include "G-d" on their websites.

While I do not propose that everyone adopt this Jewish tradition, we can learn from it. God's name is holy and must be held in high regard. However, merely treating His name (whether written or verbal) with respect is insufficient. Because His name describes His impeccable character, it must also be worshiped.

God's Name Must be Worshiped

As Christians, we can easily become involved in the experience of worship. We go to church and sing the songs we like, listen to the music we like, and sit through sermons we like. Then we leave and say that we have worshiped God. But have we?

What is worship, anyway? The Old Testament word translated in the Bible as "worship" means "to prostrate" or "do reverence."[7] It occasionally appears as "bowed," even in the act of obeisance to other people. In the New Testament, the Greek word most often translated "worship" carries the idea of a dog kissing his master's hand in anticipation of receiving attention or a handout. Specifically, it means "to fawn or crouch to."[8] Doesn't that paint a descriptive picture in your mind? Simply stated, we worship when we recognize the greatness of someone (or something). Worship of God includes much more than simply thanking Him for what He has done for us, or absentmindedly mouthing the lyrics to whatever song appears on the screen on Sunday morning. Worship recognizes and declares His embedded character. It acknowledges who He is.

How does God prefer for us to worship? Maybe we should begin with publicly proclaiming the glory of God. David declared that all nations will one day come before God and glorify His name (Psalm 86:9). Proclaiming the impeccable character of God as manifested in His names gives Him the glory He deserves. Worship is therefore much more than quiet meditation on God. Maybe that is why David called for people to praise God with all kinds of instruments, including tambourines and cymbals (Psalm 150)!

Many, of course, refuse to recognize and worship the great name of God. However, this is only a temporary situation. Every person will ultimately bow to Jesus, God in the flesh, recognizing His glory as God. In writing to the Philippians, Paul prophesied that "at the name of Jesus every knee should bow…and that every tongue should confess that Jesus Christ is Lord" (Philippians 2:10-11). So, the choice is clear. You praise God now or you praise Him later.

We may often fall prey to the notion that worship is primarily a goosebump-producing feeling of affection for God. Goosebumps are fine. However, we should also be engaged in *practical* worship. That simply means that it shows up in how we respond to the situations we face in our everyday lives. Next time you do not understand what He is doing, why don't you try to praise Him anyway? Simply let Him know that although you are confused about His plan, you are willing to submit to Him and obey anyway. That may not feel like worship, but it's the real thing.

Speaking of obeying, would you not consider obedience one of the greatest forms of worship? When I obey another person, I make it obvious that I consider him to be greater than myself. Obedience to God demonstrates my understanding that He is supreme—not just over creation as a whole, but in *my* personal life.

Why do *you* worship God? Is it because of things He has done for you or because of who He is? If you worship Him only for what He has done, how will you react when you come to one of the inevitable droughts of life? What about when you call to Him and He does not answer? How about those tumultuous times when life seems to spin violently out of control? What will you do when He allows disappointment to invade your life?

We must always remember that God is worthy of our worship whether or not we approve of what He is doing. He is worthy of our devotion and praise whether or not we understand His purposes. Yes, we can be motivated to worship even when we are miserable in our circumstances. But that is only possible when we understand that the basis for worship is His character. This character, as we will see, is revealed in His names.

Reflections on Chapter 1:
The *Worthiness* of His Name

1. For what purpose did God reveal His names to His people?

2. How did the Jews feel about the written name of God?

3. Why is it important to worship God for who He is rather than just for what He has done?

4. What does it mean to worship?

5. What are some ways that the name of God is disrespected in our society today?

6. How can you show respect to the name of God?

Chapter 2

Respect for His Name

You shall not take the name of the LORD your God in vain, for the LORD will not hold him *guiltless who takes His name in vain.*

(Exodus 20:7)

Adultery. Lies. Cover-up. Murder. Sounds like a captivating plot behind the latest blockbuster hit, doesn't it? The kind of show we probably shouldn't watch, much less allow our kids to see. Well, I'm going to let you in on a secret. *It's in the Bible.* Of course, I'm not telling you anything new. If you have spent any amount of time reading the Bible, you already knew that. Unfortunately, many people do not. Some folks actually have the audacity to claim that the Bible is boring, or even outdated. How can that be? The same characteristics that make the latest Hollywood hits successful are crammed onto almost every page from Genesis to Revelation.

For a case in point, let's look at David's not-so-secret affair with Bathsheba. When he engaged in the spontaneous rendezvous with his gorgeous neighbor, he assumed that no one would ever know. However, it wasn't long before he received some dreaded news. Bathsheba was pregnant. Questions would soon begin to fly, because Bathsheba's military husband had been deployed for quite a while. Somebody was sure to start prodding, and David's sin would become public knowledge.

That was the adultery part of the saga. Next came the lies, cover-up, and murder. David had to act decisively and quickly, as it would not be long before Bathsheba's "baby bulge" would make its appearance. To spare his reputation, he devised a brilliant scheme whereby Bathsheba's husband would be slaughtered on the battlefield. The plan worked like a charm, and David quickly invited the grieving Bathsheba into his collection of wives. For a while, everything seemed to be just fine. That is, until God described all the sordid details of the incident to the prophet Nathan. Nathan immediately confronted David and informed him of his punishment: the child that would soon be born would die.

David's response was a quick and sincere repentance of his sin. While at other times God alleviated judgment when transgressors repented, in this case He refused to do so. Why not on this occasion? Apparently David wondered the same thing, so God gave him an answer. He informed David that "because by this deed you have given great occasion to the enemies of the LORD to blaspheme, the child also who is born to you shall surely die" (2 Samuel 12:14). David had dishonored God's name before His enemies, so the punishment would not be retracted. The adultery was sin. The lies were sin. The murder was sin. However, the offense that trumped all others was that David had brought dishonor to the name of God.

Because the names of God reveal His character, we are obligated to treat them with utmost respect. We have already observed the manner in which many Jews strive to handle the name of God with care, but what about everyone else? The first thought that comes to your mind may be a phrase taken from

Exodus, which forbids taking the name of God "in vain" (Exodus 20:7). What does this phrase mean? Is it simply a reference to using God's name as an expletive, or is there something more to it?

The word translated as "take" in Exodus 20:7 signifies "lifting up"[1] an object, and is often used throughout the Old Testament to describe when one "lifts up his eyes" to look at something. It also refers to the carrying of an object. The word translated as "in vain" has some variations in meaning. It refers to wickedness, falsehood, and vanity (emptiness)[2]. Putting all this together, we could rightly say that Exodus 20:7 is a command to refrain from carrying (or bearing) the name of God in a wicked, false, or empty manner.

Now that we understand the meaning of this commandment, how should it play out practically in our daily lives? First, let's look at the most widely understood application—our speech.

Respect in our Speech

If you were to ask the average man on the street what it means to take God's name in vain, he would probably tell you that it refers to using God's name as an expletive. While we will see that the command in Exodus 20:7 carries applications far beyond speech, guidelines for the way we speak are definitely included.

Does the name of God ever come out of your mouth in a disrespectful way? We have all heard God's name used as an expression. It has become dreadfully common to hear the names of God and even Jesus Christ used in a derogatory fashion. It is becoming increasingly difficult to find television shows or movies where the name of God is treated with respect. Even children, acting on the influence of their parents or peers, blurt out the name of God carelessly to show their shock or displeasure.

Whether this is done thoughtlessly or on purpose, it makes a mockery of the holy name of God. Remember, many Jews would not even write the name of God in fear that the paper on which it was written might be treated with disrespect. Because we have no clear commandment to do likewise, is it permissible to go to the other extreme and use it carelessly? Next time you are about to use the name of God as an expression, stop and ask, "Do I really understand who He is?" If He is actually the almighty Creator of the universe who holds our lives in His hands, should we not consider speaking of Him with a greater level of respect?

Even among Christians it has become popular to use the name of God flippantly. Have you ever met someone who constantly blurts out "Bless God!" during the course of a conversation? While it may sound like "spiritual talk," is she really trying to bestow blessings on God, or is she merely attempting to fill dead time while contemplating what to say next? Using the name of God in this sloppy manner is a rejection of the respect that God demands for His name as commanded in Exodus 20:7.

Part of the definition of taking God's name in vain includes taking it falsely. Many people have unsuspectingly done this. For example, have you ever said, "I swear to God . . ." to prove some point you were trying to make? I know this seems frivolous because it is done frequently and usually in a lighthearted manner. However, are you truly prepared to swear before the God of the universe that you are going to do whatever it is you are swearing to do?

Of course, the issue of using God's name as an oath extends into the legal system. In the courtroom a witness raises his hand and swears before God that he will tell the truth, the whole truth, and nothing but the truth. Although some refuse to do this based on religious principle, I do not believe that it is wrong if you perform the oath with all seriousness and proceed to tell the truth as you have sworn to do. If you are caught lying on the witness stand, you are guilty of perjury, a very serious offense. More importantly, you are guilty before God, having solemnly offered an oath before Him, invoking His holy name. God's opinion on this matter is more fully revealed in Leviticus, where He commanded the Israelites that they should not "swear by My name falsely" or "profane the name of your God" (Leviticus 19:12). This is not a prohibition of oath-taking, but a warning that God does not take it lightly.

God Himself is known to have made oaths. Because there is no one greater than God, He swore "by Himself" (Hebrews 6:13) that He would bless Abraham and his descendants. It is not the solemn taking of an oath that is forbidden, but the breaking of the oath.

It is easy to see that we can take God's name in vain through our speech. However, there are some ways that we can take His name in vain and we may not even be aware that we are doing it. Take worship, for instance. Did you know that you can take the name of God in vain through your worship experiences?

Respect in our Worship

Most churches have what is called a "worship time" when the members meet together. Music generally is prominent during this part of the service, and that in itself leads to some difficulty. It may come as no surprise to you that music is a hot topic in Christianity today. It seems like everyone has an opinion about how much beat should be allowed in a sound track or if sound tracks should be used at all. Some argue about whether or not words to a song should be projected on a screen. In many churches, half of the crowd prefers to stick with the old hymnals, while the rest would rather chuck them into the closest trash bin and tune up their guitars for the latest praise choruses. To make matters worse, those on both sides of the argument come armed with an arsenal of Bible verses to back up their opinions. In the midst of all of this chaos, very few actually think about the songs or why they are singing them. Some piously gloat from behind their hymnals while the music director, wearing a neatly pressed suit and colorful tie, leads a "good old hymn of the faith" from the pulpit. Others follow along with their jean-clad worship leader as he croons their favorite contemporary tunes, arrogantly manifesting to the "old traditionalists" their freedom in Christ.

Has it ever crossed your mind that God may get sick of this whole debacle? That is not worship! Worship is not defined as smugly forcing upon a church our favorite style of music without thought to the feelings of others. Some worship leaders and pastors have divided their congregations by introducing music that goes against the standards of many of the members. Others have rejected newer styles and methods just because they were secretly afraid to break out of tradition. Can God be happy about all of this selfishness that takes place under the banner of His name? We are not to worship a style of music. Rather, we should worship the One whose name appears in the lyrics!

So, you may ask, what kind of music facilitates correct worship? While I wish I could say something that would end the debate once and for all, I have to admit that just like everyone else, I have my own preferences. Sometimes slow and melodious songs like "Amazing Grace" seem fitting. Is there any better way of describing the grace that God has shown to us? Other times, however, I need some good ol' Southern Gospel. The upbeat toe-tapping rhythm that facilitates rejoicing in the fact that God loves sinners can lift a soul out of any despondency. Still other times praise and worship music seems to be in order.

Did you know that you can even worship God through some

secular music? I am not referring to head-pounding reverberations that serve as a sorry excuse for music or anything vulgar or that carries an unbiblical message. However, there are some great love songs that assist you in obeying God by enhancing the relationship between you and your husband or wife. Because a strong marriage bond is part of God's plan, using music as a tool to strengthen it can be a method of worship.

While we each seem to know exactly what type of music God prefers, are we willing to let others also have their opinions and let God sort out who is actually worshiping Him? After all, which is discussed more often in the Bible—music with a little too much (or too little) beat or sowing discord among brothers? I'll let you be the judge.

We can test whether or not we are correctly worshiping God through an evaluation of our attitudes. For example, what goes through your mind when your church's music director or praise band plays a song that you deem to be "over the edge?" If you sit fuming in your pew with your lips pursed and arms folded, the chances are good that you are worshiping your own preferences instead of God. I am not saying that we should throw all music standards out the window. However, we must remember that unless a style of music is specifically forbidden in the Bible, some Christians may be able to use it to worship God.

Although music usually comes to the forefront when we hold a discussion about worship, it is only one part of the package. What may really come as a surprise to you is that it is also possible to disrespect God's name through our prayers.

Think about how you pray. When you are asked to pray in public, do you actually talk to God or to those around you who are listening in? Maybe you have watched a mother speaking to her child in the grocery store line. After little Johnny grabs a candy bar off the rack, she loudly engages in a five-minute monologue directed toward the child. It is, however, actually designed to show all the innocent (and annoyed) bystanders how this dreadful child has been the scourge of her life for the past five years. Poor little Johnny just has to stand there and accept the humiliation.

Does God ever feel like that? We burst into His house in droves every week for a party and when He meets us at the door, we throw our coats and hats on Him like He is our personal cosmic butler. Then we go have a good time without any real thoughts of Him. Sure, we chuck some token prayers His direction and occasionally reference Him in a song, but we are really there because we want to see our friends or we like the music. Or it might just be that we mindlessly attend church every Sunday simply because it has become a habit. Someone opens the service with a heartless invitation for God to "be with us in our worship today." He gets mentioned again when we're about to take up the offering, and once more when it's time to go home. But does anyone give any real thought to giving Him sincere thanks for who He is?

Respect in our Lifestyle

Remember the word "take" in "you shall not take the name of the Lord your God in vain" (Exodus 20:7) from the Ten Commandments? It refers to carrying something. The Israelites (the original recipients of the Ten Commandments) were chosen by God as missionaries who were to carry the story of His greatness into the world. That task has been temporarily re-assigned to the Church. Everywhere we go, we as Christians carry the name of God with us. We are His representatives as we go about our daily business.

How are we doing with this responsibility? Agur, writing

what we know today as the thirtieth chapter of Proverbs, was concerned with his lifestyle because of how it reflected on God. This was his request:

> *Two things I request of You*
> *(Deprive me not before I die):*
> *Remove falsehood and lies far from me;*
> *Give me neither poverty nor riches—*
> *Feed me with the food allotted to me;*
> *Lest I be full and deny You,*
> *And say, "Who is the LORD?"*
> *Or lest I be poor and steal,*
> *And profane the name of my God.*
>
> (Proverbs 30:7-9)

In these verses the phrase "profane the name of my God" is based on the same principle as taking God's name "in vain" as found in Exodus 20:7. It indicates handling something carelessly, such as when Moses threw the law-engraved tables of stone on the ground in his anger. Agur recognized that living in wickedness would bring disrespect to the name of God. He realized, like we should, that everywhere we go we are representatives of God.

What do people think about God when they observe you? The Israelites struggled with this. All of their neighbors knew that Jehovah was their God. He had miraculously brought them out of slavery in Egypt and given them the Promised Land. However, they later found themselves dispersed throughout the world, their previously majestic kingdom lying in shambles. Everywhere they went when they were scattered, people knew their story and it looked as though their God was unable to take care of them. Ezekiel verbalized God's lament that "when they came to the nations, wherever they went, they profaned

My holy name—when they said of them, 'These are the people of the LORD, and yet they have gone out of His land'" (Ezekiel 36:20). The identifying mark of the Israelites was that they served Jehovah alone while the other nations worshiped a multiplicity of gods. When the other nations observed that Israel had become powerless, they attributed it to an impotent God and "profaned" His name.

To "profane" something is to defile it. Just like the Israelites of old, we may never dream of lying under oath or using God's name as an expletive. However, our testimony can often inflict much greater damage to God's name than anything that we can say. As Christians, we represent God. When we reject His commands, we manifest to the world that we do not trust Him enough to live in obedience. Additionally, the punishment He inflicts because of sin may seem to outsiders to be a result of His inability to care for His people.

Because God is worthy of respect, it is vitally important that we treat His name honorably. However, if His worthiness does not urge us to consider how we reflect His character to the world, maybe a warning will suffice. Take another look at the end of Exodus 20:7. God will not "hold him guiltless who takes His name in vain." Those who bear God's name in a worthless manner will be pronounced as guilty. God's name represents His holy character and demands the highest respect possible.

Reflections on Chapter 2:

Respect for His Name

1. What are some ways that our society shows disrespect for the name of God?

2. What is the difference between taking God's name in vain and taking an oath in a courtroom?

3. Is it possible to worship God in a church service that is not catering to our own musical preferences?

4. How can we disrespect God through our prayers?

5. What does it mean to profane the name of God?

6. In what non-verbal ways do we profane the name of God?

Chapter 3

The *Importance* of His Name

Give unto the LORD, O you mighty ones,
Give unto the LORD glory and strength.
Give unto the LORD the glory due to His name;
Worship the LORD in the beauty of holiness.
(Psalm 29:1-2)

Have you ever struggled with what to call a particular person? As a child, my parents instilled in me the necessity of showing respect for those in authority. Every adult was a "Mr." or "Mrs." During my college years, I became friends with a faculty member. Upon my graduation, he asked me to begin calling him by his first name because I was no longer a student. However, I just could not bring myself to do that. Several years ago I came in contact with my second grade teacher who has since become a missionary. I invited her to give a presentation of her work at my church, and even then I could not bring myself to refer to her by her first name. There are also several men in my life that will always be "Pastor" to me. Although we are now colleagues, the respect factor remains.

There is (or at least should be) respect that is given to people who hold certain positions. If you received an invitation to a meeting with the president of the United States, you would be wise to employ the use of official titles. Regardless of your political leanings, you would use the title "Mr. President" or "Madame President" because of the respect the office deserves.

Is it appropriate that we treat the Supreme Being of the universe with any less respect than we would afford to another person? Usually we refer to Him simply as "God." Sometimes we call Him "Lord." There are some people who think we are not really showing respect unless we refer to Him as "Jehovah." So, what are we supposed to call Him?

In the Bible we observe three primary names of God which serve as the foundation for many of His other titles. On a day-to-day basis, the English equivalents of these primary names are the ones we use to refer to Him. Other words are added to these, forming compound words that make up His other names. In this chapter we will discuss His primary names, which are *Elohim* (God), *YHWH* (Jehovah), and *Adonai* (Lord).

Elohim – He is Supreme

The complexity of the universe requires that a powerful being has to be in control, a fact that has not been lost on humans since the beginning of time. Although many prefer to spend their lives searching for a viable explanation of how the universe can exist without the supervision of a supreme being, one cannot discount the evidence that at the very least there is an intellectual source behind everything we see. For proof, you need to look no further than your own body. For example, hold your index finger up in front of you. What do you see? Maybe you see just a finger. But do you have any idea how complex that digit is? Now take your finger and push it against something as hard as you can. Unless you are overzealous and break your finger, it probably doesn't really hurt. Now, go find a needle and lightly prick the end of your finger. You will immediately recoil in pain. Why? How can a tiny needle hurt when you barely touched it? You probably did not apply any more pressure than when you stroke your cat's fur. You certainly applied less pressure than when you pushed your finger against the hard object, yet the extremely complex system of nerves in your fingertips sent a message to your brain that your finger was in danger.

How can your brain determine the difference between a slight pin prick and hard pressure, and use the information to determine that one is dangerous while the other is not? How did you gain the ability to decipher the difference? Did it happen by accident or was it designed that way?

The complexity of the universe has prompted many people to argue over the concept of "intelligent design." An argument for intelligent design is not necessarily an argument for the existence of God. It is simply a recognition that someone or something deliberately planned for everything that we see around us to work together the way that it does.

The universe has all the indications of being intelligently designed. Paul, in fact, pointed out to the Romans that God's "invisible attributes are clearly seen, being understood by the things that are made, even His eternal power and Godhead" (Romans 1:20). To examine the universe, realizing that we are learning new things about our surroundings every day, and yet believe that it is a product of chance takes more faith than simply accepting the existence of a Creator. I recently heard someone declare, "I don't have enough faith to be an atheist." Although I cannot understand how there can be a supreme being that created and controls nature, I find that concept easier to accept than the notion that the cosmos is nothing more than a product of random chance.

Most civilizations recognize the necessity of an intelligent overseer of the universe, and therefore accept the existence of some type of supreme being or beings, known in Hebrew as *elohim*, or "gods." The word *elohim* is the plural of the Hebrew word *eloah*, which is a reference to deity. In the Bible, both the singular and plural forms of this word are used in reference to the supreme ruler of the universe, the one we know simply as "God." We will therefore capitalize this word when used in direct reference to Him.

The name *Elohim* appears in the very first verse of the Bible. The author (Moses) did not intend to engage in an argument for the existence of *Elohim*. There is no debate. God's existence was assumed when Moses wrote, "In the beginning *Elohim* created the heavens and the earth" (Genesis 1:1). He used the plural form of the word, giving insight into a truth that would not be completely understood for thousands of years: the doctrine of the Trinity. The biblical writers indicated that the Godhead consists of the Father, the Son, and the Holy Spirit. According to Moses, each took an active part in creation. At this point, however, it is sufficient to know that there is a supreme being who is responsible for forming the universe.

The first verse in the Bible provides for us an answer to the question of how creation can be so tremendously complex. Consider, for example, a computer. Most people who use a computer have no idea how it works. They turn it on and the letters they punch into the keyboard miraculously appear on the screen. They have no idea how it gets there and frankly they don't really care, at least until something does not work correctly. What happens in the mysterious "box" is beyond their comprehension. Maybe it's magic or some kind of witchcraft. It really does not matter, though, as long as it works.

The fear and awe of computers results from ignorance about

how they work. Unlike the everyday user, a computer technician understands how everything fits together. He realizes that at its core a computer is merely a machine that processes binary code, which is simply a long string of zeroes and ones generated by small electrical impulses. Everything that takes place in the microscopic circuitry of the motherboard can be explained by someone who has been trained in computer science. The intricacies of creation, however, cannot be thoroughly explained by any man. When we learn new information about our surroundings, we find ourselves continuously amazed by the delicate balance of life. We are amazed because we do not have a comprehensive understanding of it. There is one, however, who does. *In the beginning God.* He was there and created it all.

Beyond our inability to grasp the physical complexity of our bodies, we have a difficult time trying to comprehend life in general. Why are we here? What is the meaning of life? Why do we suffer? Is there any hope for the future? A search for the answers to all these questions must begin with "in the beginning God." What seems inexplicable and confusing to us poses no threat to God. As the Supreme Being of the universe, He understands not only *how* it all fits together but *why* it does. Aren't you glad that in the beginning there was a supreme being? The name *Elohim* shows us that we are much more than a product of random chance. We have been intentionally designed. If our existence was intentional, then it stands to reason that we also have both purpose and a destiny. It is this knowledge that serves as our basis for persevering through the miserable seasons of life.

Jehovah – He Exists

While the name *Elohim* describes the Supreme Being of the universe, the Creator of everything, the next name we will look at stresses the fact that He does, indeed, exist. While in English this name usually appears as Jehovah, you will often see it spelled as *Yahweh* or *YHWH*. The reason for this is that the ancient Hebrew language did not have vowels in its written form. Around the tenth century AD, the Masoretes, Jews who copied Scriptures for preservation purposes, added a system of markings into the Hebrew language to indicate the correct pronunciation of the words. Using their system of vowel markings, we know that that the correct pronunciation of this name of God is *Yahweh*. In English Bibles this name of God is typically translated as LORD (with all capital letters). To fully grasp the significance of this highly revered name, we must understand the context in which it was revealed.

The Israelites were serving in forced bondage in Egypt. It seemed to them that they were all alone, their one God having neglected them in the midst of a polytheistic society. Their forefathers had passed down the knowledge that in the past *Elohim* had spoken to Abraham and chosen him to become the patriarch of their great nation. But now look where they were! It did not seem fitting that a people who were specially chosen by *Elohim* should be experiencing such persecution. Where was *Elohim*? Did He truly exist? If He existed at all, did He care about their plight?

God had previously revealed Himself to Abraham as *El-Shaddai*, God Almighty (Genesis 17:1). If He was so mighty, why did He not utilize His power to alleviate some of their pain? This, by the way, is a common question for those who are suffering. Does God even care? Is He really out there somewhere?

As the Israelites pondered this question while laboring under the heat of the Egyptian sun, God was preparing to reveal a new aspect of His nature. Moses, an escaped convict, had secluded himself deep in the desert, content to tend sheep for his father-in-law. One day, as went about his mundane task of guiding the flock through the wilderness, he stepped aside to inspect a bush that was on fire. He cautiously approached it, curious as to why it was not being consumed. Imagine his surprise when he heard a voice. A tentative glance around proved that there was no other living being in the area except the flock of smelly sheep. He was even more astonished to find out that the voice was coming from the bush! When he came to his senses, he realized that it was the voice of God. God had come to him to assign him a new task. Moses was to resign from shepherding and return to Egypt. There he was to march right up to the king and command him to free the Israelites. Then he would lead the whole assembly out of Egypt and into a new country where they would be free. Simple task, right?

Aside from the small matter that his name appeared at the top of "Egypt's Most Wanted" list for a murder he had committed, Moses had other apprehensions about taking this job. Why would the Israelites listen to him? If he were to show up and inform them that *El-Shaddai* was going rescue them from Egypt, why would they believe him? What had *El-Shaddai* done for them in the past four hundred years? As far as they were concerned, the God of their fathers was nonexistent. Utilizing the names *Elohim* or *El-Shaddai* was definitely not going to work in this situation. Moses needed either another God or another name for God. How was he to refer to the One who had sent him to carry out this impossible task? Moses suspected that the Israelites would ask the name of the God who sent him to them, so what should He be called? The response given to him revealed a characteristic of God that the Israelites needed to know. Translated into English, it comes across as "I AM that I AM" (Exodus 3:14).

The Hebrew word translated as "I AM" is *hayah*, which simply means that He exists.[1] *Hayah* serves as the root word for the name

YHWH, or *Yahweh*, which we know as "Jehovah." This name indicates that God is self-existent. Whether or not the Israelites perceived it, their God existed.

A little while later, after Moses' first failed attempt at convincing Pharaoh to free the Israelites, God showed up again to Moses to remind him that "I am the LORD: and I appeared unto Abraham, unto Isaac, and unto Jacob, by the name of God Almighty [*El-Shaddai*], but by my name JEHOVAH was I not known to them" (Exodus 6:2-3 KJV).

We will see later in this study that the patriarchs who predated Moses were indeed familiar with the name Jehovah. Abraham had even named the altar upon which he nearly sacrificed Isaac *Jehovah-Jireh* (Genesis 22:14). This seeming contradiction is easily resolved by thinking of "knowing" in a deeper sense than simply having knowledge that the name exists. To truly know something is to know it experientially, which I think is the case here. Sure, the patriarchs and the Israelites *knew* that one of God's names was Jehovah, but their miraculous freedom from Egypt would *prove* it to them. They would know *by experience* that Jehovah did, in fact, exist.

In manifesting Himself through the name Jehovah, God was reminding His people once again that He truly exists. Remember, they were enduring great suffering and were likely questioning if He was real. He would show them that not only did He exist, but He knew about their suffering, and He was making plans to send relief.

As we continue our investigation of the names of God, we will see over and over again that He actively engages Himself in our everyday lives. Whether or not we perceive His existence, He is constantly watching us. The Israelites had undergone a four hundred year period during which they had all but given up on the existence of God. However, He had not disappeared.

At times we may also feel like we reside in Egypt. Insurmountable problems overtake us and we wonder if the God we used to know was merely a figment of our imagination or a product of our emotions. However, He has always been and will always be Jehovah, the God who exists.

Adonai – He is Lord and Master

One of the most wonderful benefits of growing up in southwest Michigan was the amount of snow that accumulated around the perimeter of the school parking lot each winter. These majestic mountains of joy provided for us a perfect venue for sledding, building forts, and everything else you could imagine. As we rolled around in the snow, oblivious to our unzipped coats and wet socks, inevitably some brazen classmate would climb to the top of the snow bank and bellow out the ultimate challenge: "I'm the king of the mountain!" Depending on who was nearby, his claim to the throne would soon be either solidified or crushed. It is natural for humans to desire greatness and control over others.

The Masters of the Universe toys were also very popular with many of my classmates. There is just something thrilling about entertaining the fantasy of becoming the supreme ruler of the cosmos. Fortunately for the rest of us, this position is already filled.

The third primary name of God causes some confusion for us. It is translated into English as "Lord," which can be used as a title for other men. However, in the Scriptures, it also serves as a proper name of God. The Hebrew word is *Adonai*, which derives from the generic title *adon*, meaning "lord" or "master." The name *Adonai* therefore illustrates the nature of God as being the true master of the universe.

Have you ever sat through an invitation in your church during which the pastor implored you to "make God the lord of your life?" While the motive behind this request is commendable, the verbiage is somewhat misleading. The name *Adonai* indicates that God *is* the lord whether or not we recognize it. We do not need to *make* Him lord of our lives; we need to *recognize* that He already is. A slave, for example, has a master whether he likes it or not. He is able to choose to either obey or disobey his master, but if he rebels he is sure to face the consequences. After he has repeatedly suffered punishment for his rebellion, he would never consider approaching his master with the promise that "I am going to put you in charge of my life." Such a statement would only invite a sneer. He *had better* recognize who is in charge if he has any inclination of avoiding punishment. The slave has no power to determine who will be his master. He retains only the ability to choose to serve willingly or unwillingly. He simply must recognize the truth of his position and live according to it.

We are not in the position to decide whether or not God will be the lord of our lives. He *is* the lord of our lives. The question is, will we accept this fact and serve willingly, or will we rebel and face the consequences? I am reminded of David's observation that "the wicked plots against the just, and gnashes him with his teeth. The Lord laughs at him, for He sees that his day is coming" (Psalm 37:12-13). For a while, it may seem as though we can get away with our sin. But we have to remember that we have a master to whom we are accountable.

In the New Testament we find a similar teaching. Paul warned us "that at the name of Jesus every knee should bow . . . and that every tongue should confess that Jesus Christ is Lord, to the glory of God the Father" (Philippians 2:10-11). As the New Testament was written in Greek, the Hebrew word *adonai*, of course, does not appear in this passage. Instead, Paul used its Greek counterpart *kurios*, which designates a supreme ruler. Although this word can, like *adonai*, be applied to other men, Jesus is different than any man. Every human being will bow to Him sooner or later and publicly recognize that He is indeed lord and master, not just of the universe, but of each individual's personal life.

Worship God for His Importance

The three primary names of God, *Elohim*, *YHWH*, and *Adonai*, demonstrate that His importance supersedes that of any other person or being in the universe. He alone is to be served and worshiped. As we will see, this applies not only to those occasions when He decides to give us what we want, but also to those times when our circumstances do not turn out exactly the way we planned. He is the supreme God who truly exists as lord and master of everything. Let us worship Him for who He is.

Reflections on Chapter 3:

The *Importance* of His Name

1. How does the universe point toward the existence of a supreme being and creator?

2. Discuss the implications of the name *Elohim*. What does it mean for us in our daily lives?

3. What is the significance of the plural word *Elohim* being used to refer to God?

4. What is the significance of Moses introducing God to the Israelites as Jehovah?

5. What is the significance in our lives of God revealing Himself as Jehovah?

6. What does the name *Adonai* suggest to us about our relationship with God?

Chapter 4

The *Power* of His Name

Is anything to hard for the LORD?
(Genesis 18:14)

The Governator. Dubya. Air Jordan. These terms may mean nothing to you. Or it is possible that just the sound of them may bring vivid memories flooding into your mind. Although these words may seem meaningless in themselves, they have been designated as nicknames for well-known people. Arnold Schwarzenegger, the actor-turned-politician, is affectionately known as the "Governator" because of his on-screen role as the Terminator. Former president George W. Bush is distinguished from his father, George H.W. Bush, by the simple fact that he has only one middle initial, a "dubya." Michael Jordan, who spent the bulk of his stellar career with the Chicago Bulls suspended in the air somewhere between the free throw line and the backboard, earned the title "Air Jordan" on account of his legendary defiance of gravity.

A nickname describes the person to whom it is attached. It conveys to the world something about him—his personality, his successes, his failures. In fact, sometimes a nickname can become so well-known that many people are not even acquainted with the real name of the person. My dad has a brother whose name, to me, was Uncle Pink. Never once in my childhood did I entertain the notion that this just might be a peculiar way to refer to a grown man. It seemed rather normal. Imagine my surprise, then, when I was in my advanced teen years and found out his real name was Sam! All of a sudden it occurred to me that I did not know many men named "Pink." Apparently when he was born ultrasounds were not available for pregnant women, and my grandmother desperately wanted a girl. As any good mother would understand, the clothes that piled up in the new baby's room were pink. So when my uncle was born, guess what color his clothes were? And the name stuck.

Do you have a nickname? If so, you are in good company. Not only do many famous people have them, but God does, too! In fact, He has several of them, and each one reveals something specific about His character.

We have already looked at the primary names of God: *Yahweh*, *Elohim*, and *Adonai*. These names are used alone in referring to God frequently throughout the Bible. However, they also are often found in conjunction with other words to illustrate some specific characteristic of God. Keep in mind that our focus should not be on what He has done for us but on His character, which is described in His names.

The first set of God's nicknames manifests His power. The Bible is jam-packed with references to the power of God. As we observed in the previous chapter, the very first verse of Scripture reveals that God created the universe. That's quite a bit of power in itself! It may be tempting, then, to think of God's power as a distant super-cosmic force that makes little difference in our daily lives. Even Abraham seemed to struggle with those feelings for a while as he waited for God to fulfill a promise He had made.

When Abraham was seventy-five years old, God had promised that his descendants would multiply into a great nation (Genesis 12:2). By the time he was eighty-five, even though God had reinforced the promise, he still was childless. Noting that his biological clock was ticking, not to mention that his wife Sarah was also sporting a few extra wrinkles, he impregnated his servant Hagar. Maybe God needed a little help in fulfilling His promise. At eighty-six years old, as a result of this union, Abraham finally celebrated the birth of a son, Ishmael (Genesis 16:13).

For thirteen years Abraham lived with the egotistical notion that he had helped God out of a bind. In his mind, although God had pledged to provide a son, He was having a little trouble bringing it about. Apparently He could not succeed without a little assistance from the wise patriarch. Nevertheless, when Abraham was ninety-nine years old, God sent an envoy to him. The messengers informed a stunned Abraham that Ishmael was, in fact, *not* the child of promise. God still planned to give the post-menopausal Sarah a child of her own. Upon hearing this, Sarah, who was eavesdropping on the conversation, could not stifle a laugh. How could she give birth to a child when she was so old? It was impossible! God, however, did not see the humor in His promise. He responded to her half-hearted inquiry with a question of His own. "Is anything too hard for the LORD?" (Genesis 18:14). Cannot the God who produced the heavens and the earth out of nothing make it possible for an old woman to become pregnant?

Sure enough, when Abraham was a centenarian and Sarah had already blown out ninety candles on her birthday cake, Isaac was made his appearance. The impossible became possible. Abraham was treated to a front-row seat for a breathtaking demonstration of the almighty power of God.

In the midst of this whole adventure, God revealed a new name to Abraham. *El-Shaddai.* The Almighty God.

El-Shaddai – The Almighty God

The name *El-Shaddai* is made up of a combination of *Elohim* (the Supreme Being) coupled with s*haddai*, which means "almighty."[1] This name first appears in the Bible when God spoke to the ninety-nine-year-old Abraham thirteen years after his illegitimate child Ishmael was born. There are several practical lessons that Abraham had to learn about *El-Shaddai* that will also benefit us if we will let them.

Lesson # 1 - He can do the impossible

For thirteen years, Abraham thought he had made God's promise possible by having an affair with Hagar. Even though he must have known that it was not right, it seemed that God had blessed the union. A son was born, and for thirteen years Abraham groomed Ishmael to be his heir. They likely developed the special bond that any father would have with his only son.

Abraham was soon to discover, however, that God needed no help in accomplishing His plans. Just as everything seemed to be moving along smoothly, all of a sudden He appeared to Abraham with the command, "I am Almighty God [*El-Shaddai*]; walk before me, and be blameless" (Genesis 17:1). In a sense He was saying, "Remember the promise I gave to you twenty-four years ago? I can make it happen without your help, because I hold all power." The impossibility for a woman of Sarah's age to procreate was irrelevant. As *El-Shaddai*, Almighty God, He could perform the impossible. He was perfectly capable of providing a son to Abraham. However, Abraham first needed a lesson in obedience.

Lesson #2 - He commands obedience

At the same time that God revealed to Abraham that He was *El-Shaddai*, Almighty God, He also commanded him to be obedient. Abraham would one day receive the elevated status of the patriarch of God's chosen people. He was therefore to obey God and cease from taking matters into his own hands. The Almighty God has the authority to demand obedience.

If you have ever held any position of leadership, you know that the authority to demand obedience is impotent without the ability to punish those who rebel. Parents especially know this firsthand. If the discussion over spanking was around when I was a child, someone forgot to tell my parents. They never wasted any time imploring us to conform to their wishes. They simply demanded that we obey, and when we chose not to, the "board of education" would be immediately, firmly, and repetitively applied to our "seats of understanding." In our house, the weapon of choice was a wooden spoon. My parents learned quickly that if we were engaging in intellectual conversation (which is exactly what it was) when we should have been sleeping, all they had to do was rattle the silverware drawer that housed the wooden saber. It may as well have been the roar of a ravenous tiger being set free from its cage judging by the quieting effect it had on us. There would be no discussions and no begging. The choice to continue in our disobedience was a choice to invite chastisement.

My children have also learned to fear the rattle of the silverware drawer. Recently as I was putting up Christmas decorations, I engaged in my annual struggle with malfunctioning lights. Three-year-old Braden was sitting on the floor playing with houses from our Christmas village. Fearing that the fragile decorative houses would soon be shattered, I told him that he was not allowed to carry them into the other room. Then I immediately went into the kitchen to find a small knife to use in removing the fuse from a reprobate strand of lights. When I returned to the living room, my uncharacteristically silent son scrutinized me carefully, his large eyes open much wider than normal. Finally, with his eyes fixated on the knife, he quietly stated, "That's not a paddle." When I realized that he had heard the rattle of the drawer and thought I was fetching an instrument of discipline, I asked him if he deserved to be spanked. He looked at me with gigantic eyes and in guarded relief replied softly, "You scared me a lot a couple." Apparently the tradition continues.

Several years ago, as I was discussing parental punishment with my mother, she informed me that she punished her children because she wanted us to experience firsthand the painful repercussions of sin. Why does sin hurt? It hurts because *El-Shaddai*, who has the authority to command obedience, backs it up with chastening.

Lesson #3 - He chastens

Everyone can identify in some way with Job. This man whose terrifying biography appears in the Old Testament experienced difficulties far beyond what any of us will ever know. We may tend, however, to trivialize his sufferings because we know that their purpose was to prove Job's dedication to God. We also know that everything came out fine in the end. Job, however, was in a fog. For all he knew, he could have been experiencing chastisement for some unknown sin. This certainly was the opinion of his friend Eliphaz, who pointed out in his misguided monologue that "happy is the man whom God corrects" followed by a command to "not despise the chastening of the Almighty" (Job 5:17). We know that Eliphaz was mistaken in his assessment of the situation, but he did understand that God holds His people to a high standard. The Almighty (*shaddai*) does indeed punish wrongdoers.

Lesson #4 - He is in control of all things

Of the forty-eight times that the word *shaddai* (whether or not it is used as a name of God) is found in Scripture, thirty-one are located in the book of Job. The beauty of this narrative is that in it we are treated to a birds-eye view of Job's seemingly desperate situation. We get to view it all from beginning to end. We know that Job's suffering came about because God was proving that Job loved Him regardless of his circumstances. We get to see Job's response to his predicament as well as the final blessings that God granted him as a result of his suffering. Although Job did not understand at the time what was taking place, God did. He knew what *had* happened, what *was* happening, and what *would* happen. Furthermore, it was all taking place under His sovereign direction. This should give us an indication of what we are supposed to learn through Job's story. No matter how hopeless our situation, *El-Shaddai* is still in control.

At certain times in our lives, we may feel like Job. It may seem that we have been alienated by God and misunderstood by the world. However, we must come to the realization that just as God was in ultimate control of Job's situation, He is also in control of ours.

Lesson #5 - He offers protection

I have no idea how many times I have been startled awake in the dead of night by the piercing scream of a child. The frantic call for "Daddy!" that penetrates the darkness is one that no parent can ignore. When a terrified child wakes up shaking on account of a terrifying dream, she immediately seeks the comfort of her parents. Even though she is only half awake, she knows where she is safe. Mommy and Daddy are big, strong, and wise. They symbolize protection. In their presence, the monsters that seemed so real fade back into the distant confines of dreamland. All is well in Daddy's arms.

As adults, we also occasionally need to run to a safe place. Where can we go to find protection? Who is bigger, wiser, and stronger than we are? How about *El-Shaddai*, the Almighty God? The biblical promise is that "he who dwells in the secret place of the Most High shall abide under the shadow of the Almighty [*Shaddai*]" (Psalm 91:1).

David, while hiding in a cave to spare his life from King Saul's wrath, wrote a prayer in which he promised God that "in the shadow of Your wings I will make my refuge, until these calamities have passed by" (Psalm 57:1). The picture he paints is that of a large bird spreading her protective wing over her young until the threat of danger fades away. Regardless of how "big and bad" we may think we are, often the pressures of the world require that we retreat to the safety of *El-Shaddai*.

El-Elyon – The Most High God

Let's look once again at Psalm 91:1, which assures us that "he who dwells in the secret place of the Most High shall abide under the shadow of the Almighty." We know that "Almighty" is translated from the Hebrew word *Shaddai*, but who is the "Most High?" If you were reading this verse in Hebrew, you would see here the word *Elyon*, which describes something that is elevated or lofty. The "Most High" is the God who is elevated above all others. That He holds such a place of pre-eminence demonstrates several more of His characteristics.

He is prominent over all

We first see the word *Elyon* used in reference to God during Abraham's encounter with a mysterious priest identified as Melchizedek. This meeting took place because Abraham's nephew, Lot, had been living in Sodom when the city was attacked by a coalition of neighboring kings. Upon receiving word that Lot had been kidnapped, Abraham mustered an army and rescued him along with the other captives from Sodom. On his return trip, he took a detour to Salem (which would later be named Jerusalem), where he met up with Melchizedek.

Our lack of knowledge about Melchizedek causes him to be surrounded with an undeniable mystique. All we know for sure is that he was a priest of "God Most High" (Genesis 14:18). This phrase is translated from a combination of *El* (the Supreme Being) and *Elyon*. The significance of describing Melchizedek's God in this way is that polytheism was the order of the day. Just as Abraham's family had served a multiplicity of gods, the Canaanites who lived in the area did also. Yet, amidst the plethora of false gods there was Melchizedek, a priest who served the *El-Elyon*, the God who is elevated above all others. Recognizing *El-Elyon* as the one true God, Abraham set apart a tenth of all the spoil he had taken in the battle and presented it to Melchizedek. He realized that the one powerful God, the Most High, inhabits a place of power above all other gods.

The fact that Moses gave a tenth of his spoil to God's priest should not be overlooked, even though it may make us uncomfortable. For some reason, it is difficult to give up our possessions. How many times have you heard a disgruntled church member claim that his pastor "always" or "only" talks about money? While this may true for some, could it be that these complaints arise because we are holding a little too tightly to what the Bible calls "unrighteous mammon" (Luke 16:11)? Maybe if we would recognize that God is *El-Elyon*, the Most High, we would understand that He is deserving of not only a tenth of our income, but all we have.

He is worthy of praise

David also recognized that *Elyon* was worthy of adoration. He promised to "tell of all your marvelous works" and "sing praise to Your name, O Most High [*Elyon*]" (Psalm 9:1-2). God can do marvelous works because He is the Most High. For that alone He is worthy of our praise.

He hears our cries

While David recognized that *Elyon* was worthy of praise, he also was aware that he could call out to Him when he was in trouble. As he was forced to camp out in a cave to spare his life from the vengeful Saul, he exclaimed, "I will cry out to God Most High [*El-Elyon*]; to God who performs all things for me" (Psalm 57:2). If He is the Most High, then He has power over all— even the greatest difficulties that come our way. We possess the unfathomable privilege of calling on the One who can perform anything. Does that make you appreciate the power of prayer just a little bit more?

He sees all

Another psalmist followed David's lead in referring to *Elyon*. In Psalm 73, Asaph lamented over his observation that the wicked seem not only to get away with their transgressions, but they prosper while doing so. Their riches increase and they escape the consequences of their sinful actions. They find such freedom in their wickedness that they even ask if God the "Most High" can see them. They inquire, "How does God know? And is there knowledge in the Most High?" (Psalm 73:11). They suppose they are getting away with their sin because God cannot see them. Asaph took issue with this arrangement because, in his words, "I have cleansed my heart in vain" (Psalm 73:13). In other words, "What do I gain by doing what is right when others get away with their sin?"

Do you ever feel like Asaph? We might ask questions like, "How come I am a good parent and active in my church, but I lose my job on the same day that my deadbeat neighbor gets a promotion?" Or, "Why did the drunk driver walk away from the wreck that killed my child?" These are the kinds of questions that have been asked since humans walked the earth. While I cannot prove it, I suspect that Adam and Eve may have secretly questioned why their rebellious son lived while the obedient one was murdered. Life just is not fair!

Why do the wicked prosper while the righteous are left to navigate through a life of exasperating hurdles? This was a painful question for Asaph, and it may be just as painful for us. However, in the end, Asaph found an answer to his dilemma. He finished the chapter by describing how God will utterly destroy the wicked. It may appear that they are getting away with their sin for the present, but their day will come. After all, the Most High God, *Elyon*, can see everything! He will not permit sin to continue indefinitely.

He requires obedience

We can be assured, along with Asaph, that God will hold man responsible for his sin. Later in Psalms we see once again what happens to people who rebel against the Most High. They "sat in darkness and in the shadow of death, bound in affliction and irons—because they rebelled against the words of God, and despised the counsel of the Most High" (Psalm 107:10-11). This pronouncement immediately follows the observation that God "satisfies the longing soul, and fills the hungry soul with goodness" (Psalm 107:9). Can you see the contrast? It may seem for a while that sinners are getting away with their wickedness, but we can be assured that the Most High God, *El-Elyon*, is watching. He sits as the ultimate judge and will hold man accountable for his actions.

Worship God for His Power

The names *El-Shaddai* and *El-Elyon* demonstrate the vast power of God. Would this not be the God that we want to worship—the One to whom we are ultimately accountable, and the One who sees all that we do? While it may seem at times that worshiping Him is pointless or even detrimental to our well-being, we can be assured that, in the end, He will honor those who serve Him and punish those who do not. We worship Him, then, by living in obedience even when we fail to see the short term benefits of doing so.

Since worship is ascribing worth to someone, we can worship God when we pray, having faith that He holds the power to grant our requests. A child honors his parents by coming to them with his needs. He acknowledges his own incapability and recognizes his need for his parents. We also are often faced with seemingly impossible situations, but when we bring these to God with faith that He has the power to intervene, we offer Him the worship that He deserves.

Reflections on Chapter 4:

The *Power* of His Name

1. How did Abraham show his lack of understanding of God's power through the births of Ishmael and Isaac?

2. Why should the fact that God is referred to as *El-Shaddai* prompt us to obey?

3. What is the significance of the repeated use of the word *shaddai* in the book of Job?

4. What do we learn from the fact that Melchizedek is referred to as the priest of *El-Elyon*?

5. What difference did *Elyon* make in the life of David?

6. What does the name *Elyon* teach us about those who seem to be getting away with their sin?

7. How should the names *El-Shaddai* and *El-Elyon* affect our worship of God?

Chapter 5

The *Presence* of His Name

For thus says the High and Lofty One
Who inhabits eternity, whose name is Holy:
"I dwell in the high and holy place,
With him who has a contrite and humble spirit,
To revive the spirit of the humble,
And to revive the heart of the contrite ones.

(Isaiah 57:15)

It does not take long trying to live as a Christian in this world before you realize that not everyone supports your lifestyle. Some of your friends may be opposed to everything you believe and claim that there is no God at all, or that if there is one, He is indifferent to us. Others concede the existence of God, but claim that we cannot know Him. Still others emphatically reject the God of the Bible, electing to serve other gods, real or imaginary. As a result, you may repeatedly come in contact with people whose worldview is radically different than yours. What can you do to keep faithful to your God without squandering the remainder of your days as a recluse in a deserted monastery? Well, it just so happens that we have an excellent example of how Abraham dealt with a similar situation. His response will introduce us to the next name of God.

We join Abraham in the land of Gerar. Having been called by God to forsake his homeland and venture into a faraway territory, he is heading toward Canaan. While he did not realize it at the time, for the rest of his life he would live as a nomad in this foreign land, building great wealth, but having no permanent home.

It was during his time in Gerar that his promised son Isaac was born. Soon after, Abimelech, the king of Gerar, began to notice how greatly God had blessed Abraham. Recognizing that it would be disastrous for Abraham to become his enemy, he offered to make a covenant of peace with him (Genesis 21:23). The king kindly reminded Abraham about the warm welcome he had received in Gerar, and indicated that he would like to see Abraham return the favor in the future to his descendants. Abraham was more than willing to agree to the covenant of peace, but he had a little issue that needed to be settled first. Apparently Abimelech's men had taken over one of Abraham's wells. Wells were prized possessions because of the extremely hot and dry climate, so to steal rights to a well was viewed as a serious crime. Abimelech pleaded innocence about the situation, so the two men made an oath recognizing Abraham's ownership of the well in question. As was customary, Abraham then conferred upon the disputed well a name that not only described its history, but would encourage the next guy to think twice before trying to steal it. He christened it Beersheba, which means "well of an oath."[1]

After settling the matter of the well's ownership and establishing a peace treaty, Abimelech departed for home, while Abraham and his entourage continued to camp around the well. One of his first activities was to plant a "grove" (Genesis 21:33 KJV). Many modern Bible versions render this as a "tamarisk tree" rather than a "grove" because the Greek word can describe either a single tree or a collection of trees. It appears likely, however, that Abraham planted a small group of trees to provide a place where he could pray to God in private.

As a side note, you may recall reading later in the Old Testament that whenever the Israelites decided to start obeying God, they would cease idol worship and cut down the "groves." This is a different word than the one used to describe Abraham's grove. It is the word *asherah*, which was also the name of a goddess whose likeness was often carved out of a tree trunk. The idol that depicted her, as well as the place where she was worshiped, became known as *asherah*. Abraham, however, planted an *eshel* rather than an *asherah*. He was not worshiping a false god. He designed this place for the purpose of worshiping the one true God. When everything was set up, he "there called on the name of the LORD, the Everlasting God" (Genesis 21:33), which introduces us to the next name in our study.

El-Olam – The Everlasting God

You will notice that in Genesis 21:33, Abraham called on the "name of the LORD" (Jehovah). However, Jehovah is also called by another name. Translated as "Everlasting God" in English, the Hebrew reads *El Olam*. *El*, which refers to a supreme being, is paired in this case with *olam*, the Hebrew word that means "eternal."[2]

Abraham, at this time, was living among polytheistic people. They worshiped a large number of gods without recognizing the existence of one superior God. Abraham, however, believed in one eternal God. Although he lived among pagans, he refused to allow their influence to affect how he worshiped. He set up a grove that would serve as his personal place to worship God.

I am not necessarily recommending that you plant an orchard in your back yard so you can pray out of earshot of your neighbors. I am suggesting, however, that you follow Abraham's example and do something that will prompt you to habitually worship God, even when it is not popular among your peers. Abraham obviously felt like he could worship God best in the woods, and because there were none available, he made his own. It may be necessary for you to designate a place in your house or your office where you know you can worship God freely. Why don't you "plant a grove" somewhere so you do not neglect to worship God?

Maybe it is not a place that you need, but a regularly scheduled time with God. For years I have made it a habit to take a walk on Saturday night to prepare myself for Sunday. I find myself looking forward to these times so much that it does not matter what the weather is like. I have walked through hot and freezing temperatures, rain, and snow. It is a time that I have built into my schedule to pray. Do you need to find a place on your schedule to "plant a grove" like Abraham did?

If you just plan to spend time worshiping God when you feel like it or get around to it, you will likely find that it never happens. If you are a morning person, get up before everyone else while the house is still quiet. Maybe you are a night owl with secret doubts that that the sunrise even exists. In that case, try dedicating yourself to spending time with God after the kids are in bed and have already asked for their final drink of water. Making this time a priority is crucial because you are worshiping the one true eternal God in a land whose inhabitants do not believe in Him. If you do not proactively engage in worship, you will find yourself serving the gods of those around you. The eternal God is the one who deserves your worship.

Although Abraham's use of *olam* is the first time this Hebrew word is applied as a name of God, it can be found 413 times throughout the Old Testament. For example, in Genesis 9:16, God provided the rainbow as the sign of an "everlasting" covenant that He would never again destroy the earth with a flood. In Genesis 17:7, the covenant that God made with Abraham is designated as "everlasting." The mercies of God are also described as "everlasting" in Psalm 100:5. God seems very fond of the idea of eternality. He alone is everlasting, having no beginning and no end. For that alone He is to be worshiped.

That God is everlasting means that He has traits that we do not possess as humans. The prophet Isaiah pointed out many of these traits in chapter forty of the book that bears his name. Like Abraham, he used the name *El-Olam* in reference to God.

In verse eighteen, Isaiah posed the question, "To whom then will you liken God? Or what likeness will you compare to Him?" That's a good question. If God is everlasting, how can any mortal being compare to Him? If we cannot compare to Him, then on what basis do we reject His wishes in favor of our own? Why do we depend on our own strength first when we are in trouble? Why do we go running to others when we need something and never consider asking God for it? If He is everlasting, why do we treat Him as insignificant by the way we conduct our daily lives? In verse twenty-five, Isaiah passed along a similar question, this time asked by God Himself. "To whom then will you liken Me, or to whom shall I be equal?" If no one is equal to God, He is unsurpassed in power. Would that not be reason enough to merit our worship?

The practicality of the fact that God is everlasting becomes evident a few verses later when the Israelites are asked why they thought their ways were hidden from God.

Why do you say, O Jacob,
And speak, O Israel:
"My way is hidden from the LORD,
And my just claim is passed over by my God?"
Have you not known?
Have you not heard?
The everlasting God, the LORD,
The Creator of the ends of the earth,
Neither faints nor is weary.
His understanding is unsearchable.

(Isaiah 40:27-28)

Although this question is specifically directed toward the Israelites, I think it would be fitting for us to contemplate it also. How is it that we do not think that God knows what we are doing? Do we really suppose that we can get away with sin without Him knowing about it?

When I was a child, I would often go to spend time at my grandparents' house. For a short period of time a cousin that I barely knew lived with them. During his stay, I was once invited to spend the afternoon with him. After considering all the options available to us, we came to an agreement on a game to play. Although I briefly thought it curious that he wanted to set up the game behind a large recliner, I did not give it much thought. That is, until Grandma found us. In my ignorance I did not know that she had banned him from that game earlier in the day for reasons that were never explained to me. Yet he thought that if we hid ourselves out of sight we could do whatever we wanted. Little did he know that it was impossible to escape the all-seeing eyes of Grandma.

If we cannot hide our actions from another person, what makes us think we can conceal ourselves from the omniscient

God? Through the prophet Jeremiah, God asked a couple of rhetorical questions. "Can anyone hide himself in secret places, so I shall not see him?" (Jeremiah 23:24). Lest our rebellion should lead us to contemplate seeking out a place in which we can hide from God, He follows up with another question. "Do I not fill heaven and earth?" God is not limited to a certain time or place. As an omnipresent spirit, He can be everywhere at once.

Next time you venture into a public place, look for signs warning that your actions may be caught on film. Security cameras are everywhere. I don't mean to make you paranoid, but we are under observation more than we would like to realize. However, even in places cameras cannot reach, we are under the observation of the omniscient Creator of the universe.

I find it comical to watch church services that are broadcast on television. Often as the cameramen pan the audience they inevitably capture an image of a poor parishioner who is having a difficult time staying attentive. He may be yawning or looking around, oblivious to the fact that his every movement is on display for the whole world to see. The glassy eyes of others in the pews indicate that they are lost in a good daydream. The real comedy begins when the inattentive person suddenly realizes that a camera is trained on him. He freezes in sheer panic, then instantly feigns intense interest in whatever the preacher is saying. If a video camera has that kind of effect on a person, should not the realization that God is watching elicit a similar response?

Knowing that God has us under surveillance should instill a sense of fear within us. After all, He sees everything that we do and think. However, on a positive note, consider that the all-seeing God also knows about your troubles and has the ability to help. Not only is He never "asleep at the wheel," but "His understanding is unsearchable" (Isaiah 40:28). In other words, try as hard as you like, but you will never begin to comprehend

His infinite intelligence. He not only knows *what* your problem is, but He knows *why* you have it and *how* to fix it.

Do you have any idea how many people are in the world today? It is estimated that over seven billion people are alive right now. That's a lot of people. Can you imagine trying to keep track of all of them? It is taxing enough to know what each of my four children are up to at any given time.

Shortly after our third child was born, I was asked to speak, along with another local pastor, in a funeral for one of our church members. The funeral was being held in our church building on a Sunday afternoon, which left little time to get back to the church after entertaining a visiting missionary for lunch. Consequently, we were running late, so as we entered the parking lot, I slowed down just enough so my wife, Lori, could jump out and sprint to her place at the piano. I then parked my van in the correct position behind the hearse, helped my older boys get situated where I hoped they couldn't cause too much of a commotion, and finally breathlessly sank into my chair on the platform. When my wife finished her prelude, she left the piano and made her way out of the sanctuary to look after our infant daughter. As my fellow preacher stood at the pulpit sharing his memories of the deceased, I noticed my wife appear in the doorway with a confused look on her face. Having both previously served as interpreters for the deaf, we can communicate quietly when necessary. She stepped in the door and signed to me, "Where's Chloe?" *Chloe? Hmm...I don't remember the last time I saw her!* The most obvious place she could be was in my office, so I instructed Lori to look there. As soon as she disappeared around the corner, it hit me. In my rush, I had neglected to get my little girl out of the car! Worse yet, I remembered the only set of keys we had with us was in my pocket. With all the funeral-worthy respect that I could gather, I slowly strolled to the back of the auditorium and humbly handed the keys to my wife. Fortunately, she found our sweet baby contentedly sleeping in her seat. Until the day I left town, the funeral directors never let me forget that humiliating experience.

If a loving father who is running late can inadvertently leave his daughter in the car, are we not all in danger of becoming so busy that some very important things can be overlooked? We may be tempted then to think that God is similarly busy and does not have time for each of us. How could He possibly care about our comparatively insignificant and mundane problems when there could be over seven billion people clamoring for His attention at any given moment? Not to mention that He also takes responsibility for the snails in the sea, the birds in the air, and the global weather patterns. If we were to truly question His ability to care for each person, then we might as well strip Him of His name. However, He is *El-Olam*, the everlasting God. Being everlasting, he has no limitations of space and time. The promise at the end of Isaiah 40 can then be applied to everyone. You may have memorized this verse or learned it in a song:

> *They that wait upon the LORD shall renew their strength;*
> *they shall mount up with wings as eagles; they shall run,*
> *and not be weary; and they shall walk, and not faint.*
> (Isaiah 40:31 KJV)

This principle also carries over into the New Testament, where we are encouraged to "not be weary in well doing; for in due season we shall reap, if we faint not" (Galatians 6:9 KJV). We have a God who not only knows everything we do, but also holds the power to provide rewards for our labor.

Jehovah-Shammah – The Lord is There

The Old Testament prophet Ezekiel lived in the day when the Babylonians destroyed Jerusalem and took the Israelites captive. While others found this to be quite a distressing event, Ezekiel was privy to some inside information that nurtured hope in his heart. God had informed him that although the future of Israel was looking rather bleak, she would one day re-establish herself as a nation and the flattened Temple would be rebuilt.

As we eavesdrop on Ezekiel's prophecy, we find that he had been treated to some specific information about Jerusalem as it would be at the time of its restoration. In the final verse of his book he declared that the city would be called *Jehovah-Shammah*. This Hebrew phrase appears in English as "the LORD is there" (Ezekiel 48:35), because the word *shammah* means simply "there."[3] The resurrected Jerusalem will be impressive not because of its architecture or economy, but because the LORD will be there in person.

What makes Ezekiel's prophecy more interesting is that its fulfillment is still future. He prophetically described Jerusalem as it will be known in the Millennium, which is the one thousand year reign of Christ on the earth after the Tribulation. During this era of peace Satan will finally be bound and imprisoned so he cannot cause trouble, and Jesus Himself will personally reign from Jerusalem. Quite literally, the LORD will be there.

The Israelites had reason to believe that God had forsaken them. Unfortunately, to a degree, it was true. Because of their sin, God had removed His protective hand from their nation. However, this was a temporary situation. They will one day again enjoy His presence.

Sometimes it is easy to think that God has forgotten all about us. Could He really be interested in what is happening every day in our lives? Maybe you can accept the idea that He created the world, but you struggle with the notion that He cares about the trials you face on a daily basis. You are not alone. In fact, scholars have even coined a theological term for this—deism. Deism is the belief that God created the world and set the processes of nature in motion, but then took His hands off it and is disinterested in what happens. The truth is, however, that God wants us to realize that He is present and active in the world. After all, if He was not concerned about what happens every day, He surely would not be making plans to come back to rule the earth. Although we cannot see Him, He is watching over everything that takes place, and He is intimately involved in it.

We have already looked at the rhetorical questions God posed through the prophet Jeremiah. He asked, "Am I a God near at hand . . . and not a God afar off? Can anyone hide himself in secret places, so I shall not see him . . . do not I fill heaven and earth?" (Jeremiah 23:23-24). Although He transcends the earth, He is right here with us. He is not so busy maintaining the universe that He cannot take time to care about us individually. In fact, He cares so much that He has allotted Himself one thousand years in which He will come to personally reign on this earth.

Worship God for His Presence

Do you ever feel like God is not there? Because we cannot see Him, we may often feel like we have been abandoned, left to navigate the treacherous minefields of life alone. You may have heard the story about the little boy who was asked to go out onto the back porch of his country home at night to fetch the broom. Because it was so dark, he hesitated in the doorway. His mother instructed him from across the room, "Don't be afraid. Jesus is out there." The little boy, eyes wide with fear, whispered out the doorway, "Jesus, if you're really out there, hand me the broom, will ya?"

How do we know that He is here with us? Our inability to see Him with our physical eyes requires that we observe Him through eyes of faith. He has promised to be with us. In fact, the last thing Jesus said before He left earth was "I am with you always, even to the end of the age" (Matthew 28:20). Being the everlasting God, without limitations, He is able to make good on His promise.

Before we finish this chapter, let's look at one more verse from Isaiah.

> For thus says the High and Lofty One who inhabits eternity, whose name is Holy: "I dwell in the high and holy place, with him who has a contrite and humble spirit, to revive the spirit of the humble, and to revive the heart of the contrite ones.
>
> (Isaiah 57:15)

God "inhabits eternity," yet He enters into time and space to dwell with those who possess a humble spirit. The everlasting God cares about mortal man. Should that alone not merit our worship?

Reflections on Chapter 5:
The *Presence* of His Name

1. How did Abraham deal with worshiping the one true God in a land where people worshiped many gods?

2. How can you set up your own "grove" to facilitate worship to God?

3. How should the name *El-Olam* prompt us to worship God?

4. What are the positives and negatives about God's ability to see and know everything?

5. What does God's future involvement with Israel teach us about how God cares for us?

6. Why is faith necessary when considering the fact that God is always with us?

Chapter 6

The *Provision* of His Name

And my God shall supply all your need according
to His riches in glory by Christ Jesus.

(Philippians 4:19)

The reality television obsession of recent years has spawned
many creative programs. Among these is the somewhat popular
Undercover Boss. In the show, the CEO of a large organization goes
undercover in his own company, posing as an entry-level worker
who is competing against other contestants for a job. The boss
is coincidentally (but predictably) paired with an overworked
and underpaid employee who typically suffers from a deeply
emotional personal history. Maybe it's a single mom struggling
to balance two jobs just to make ends meet, or a promising
young man who has been repeatedly stripped of opportunities for
success. Although the story lines are very similar in each of the
episodes, the interest lies in the fact that when the boss reveals his
true identity, the employees know that he has finally experienced
the reality of everyday life in the company. He has descended
from his perch in a comfortable office to get his hands dirty. He
has lived a day in the trenches. To add to the drama of the story,

the incognito CEO often bungles his tasks, unable to adequately learn his job. In the end, he offers worthy subordinates such rewards as paid schooling, promotions, or vacations. He claims to finally understand what it is like to work in his business. He has seen the needs of the employees firsthand and knows better what he can do to help them.

While God does not have to star in a reality show on network television to understand what life is like for us, He does see all we do. That is what we will discover in His next name.

El-Roi – The God Who Sees

The name *El-Roi* should capture our interest because it appears on the lips of an unlikely source, one who was neither a patriarch nor an Israelite. Rather, a desperate Egyptian slave named Hagar saw something in the character of God that caused her to refer to Him in this way.

As we discussed earlier, God had promised a son to Abraham. However, when He delayed fulfilling His promise, Abraham figured it would be best to take matters into his own hands. His impatience caused him to doubt God's ability to provide what He had promised, so he had an affair with his wife's servant. When this union resulted in the birth of a son, Abraham perceived that he had done what was right. Surely, in his mind, the end justified the means. Although Sarah had consented to the affair and had even recommended it, Abraham had been unfaithful to his wife. Any guilt he may have had, however, faded away with the conviction that he had facilitated the implementation of God's will.

I realize that this incident may seem a little strange. A woman encourages her husband to have an affair? That is ridiculous! It may help a little to gain an understanding of how women in

Abraham's culture determined their social status. While we are accustomed to women searching for their worth on the higher rungs of the corporate ladder, women in biblical times were defined by their children. To be childless was shameful. When Hager conceived, she instantly became socially superior to her mistress, which caused Sarah to be "despised in her eyes" (Genesis 16:4). The master-servant relationship had been jeopardized, and the humiliation proved too much for Sarah. After receiving permission from Abraham, she treated Hagar with such severity that the pregnant woman decided to escape into the wilderness.

That is where we find Hagar. She is trudging through the wilderness; pregnant, alone, and frightened. She had, after all, been taken into a foreign land as a servant. What would she do now? Where could she go? We are not told if she had been a willing accomplice in Abraham's sin, but most likely her opinion did not matter, anyway. Abraham was the master; she was the servant. She must do as she was commanded. Now, as a result of the indiscretion of an impatient master, she must spend her days as a vagabond with no hope for the future.

As an Egyptian, Hagar probably believed in a multiplicity of gods. As a servant to the monotheistic Abraham, she would have heard that there was only one true God. Well, where was this God? If He truly existed, had He forgotten about her? Maybe He was God only to Abraham and not to anyone else. Did He care that she had been mistreated and abandoned? Did it matter to Him that she would need nourishment not only for herself, but also for her child? What would she do when it came time for delivery? Without answers, she did the only thing she knew to do. She headed home.

Genesis 16:7 tells us that Hager set up camp near a fountain of water on the way to Shur. While we cannot be certain of the exact location of Shur, we know that the Israelites arrived there soon after crossing the Red Sea in the exodus from Egypt (Exodus 15:22). The Bible also refers to Shur as being "east of Egypt" (Genesis 25:18). Evidently Shur was close to the border of Egypt, indicating that Hagar was indeed on her way home. Where else would we expect her to go?

Although life seemed hopeless for Hagar, God had not abandoned her. While she was resting at the fountain, an angel of God appeared and instructed her to return and submit herself to Sarah. The angel also informed her that she would have a son and must name him Ishmael, which means "God will hear."[1] Her son would forever serve as a reminder that God had heard the desperate cries of her affliction. I imagine that as this young, homeless, pregnant woman wandered through the desert, she cried out to every god she could remember. The real God heard her. She would not die in the wilderness. She would give birth to her son, and although he would develop into "a wild man," from him would come a nation of innumerable people.

Now Hagar could be assured of the existence of Abraham's God. He had revealed Himself in an undeniable way. When she thought she was all alone in the midst of her distress, He had seen her. *Elohim*, the supreme being of the universe, had His eyes on her. For Hagar, simply calling Him *Elohim* was no longer sufficient. He was more than the distant and disinterested CEO of the universe. He was not just *God*, but *the God who sees me*. As a result, she called Him *El-Roi*, "you are the God who sees" (Genesis 16:13). What a surprise to realize that God was watching her! Furthermore, she decided to rename the well where she had been staying. She dubbed it *Beer-Lahai-Roi*, which means "well of the living one who sees me."[2]

One evening as I was in the basement of our house, I heard an awful racket on the stairs, followed by the half-scared-half-hurt cry of my youngest son. I rushed to the scene and immediately sized up the situation. Apparently a blanket, sippy cup, and armful of toys was too much of a load for a two-year-old who was just learning to negotiate stairs. He had landed about four steps from the bottom with half of his body dangling off the edge, a small gash in his forehead, and a look of terror in his eyes. Fortunately for him, Daddy was able and willing to come to the rescue. To leave a child in such a predicament would have been unthinkable. I saw his problem and I saved him out of it. I was the hero.

The fact that God sees us would be unimpressive if He ignored our plight. If He would have observed Hagar's trouble in the wilderness but refused to help her, she would have taken no comfort in His omniscient vision. However, He not only was able to *see*, but He was also willing (and able) to *provide*. This leads us to the next name that we will discuss. Although it is often thought of as a name for God, it is never attributed to Him, but rather to an altar.

Jehovah-Jireh – Jehovah Sees

We now skip forward several years to after the birth of Isaac, the son originally promised to Abraham and Sarah. Keep in mind that Abraham had been guaranteed by God that Isaac was the promised son through whom would come a very large nation. As the child grew, Abraham could look forward to the day when Isaac would provide him with grandchildren, and he would begin to see God's plan begin to take shape. One day, however, God put Abraham's faith to the test. He commanded Abraham to take his beloved son Isaac up a mountain in the land of Moriah and offer him as a sacrifice on an altar.

I distinctly remember the day my first child was born. There is nothing that can compare to seeing the first glimpse of your child and realizing, "I'm a daddy now!" Until that time, I never really grasped the love a father has for his son. I knew that I would protect this boy with my life. Nothing would hurt him if I had anything to say about it. I can only imagine, then, what Abraham thought when God commanded him to offer Isaac as a sacrifice. Although we are not told if Abraham questioned God at this time, I surmise that they had a discussion that has not been recorded for us. I know that I would have required some kind of miraculous proof that I truly understood God's command. No doubt Abraham felt the same way.

Satisfied that he was in possession of a clear directive from God, Abraham obediently rolled out of bed early in the morning and started off with Isaac on a three day journey toward the specified mountain. When they approached the place God had designated, he left his servants behind, informing them that he and Isaac "will go yonder and worship, and we will come back to you" (Genesis 22:5). Although God had directed him to offer his son as a sacrifice, he knew they would both return. God had made an oath. Isaac would have descendants. Regardless of what happened on the mountain, Isaac would be alive at the end of the day.

The details of what transpired on that mountain can only be imagined. When did Isaac realize that he was to be the sacrifice? How willing was he to go along with the plan? How long did it take Abraham to muster up the courage to bind his son? We can only speculate, but clearly Abraham had every intention of going through with the sacrifice. At the last second, however, God intervened. God did not stop him as he was heading toward the mountain or as he was building the altar. God silently observed as Abraham tied up Isaac and boosted him onto the kindling. It was not until Abraham had the knife in his hand, ready to plunge it into his son, that his faith was confirmed.

Just as Abraham was about to take the life of his only son, God stopped him with the command to do nothing to harm the boy, for "now I know that you fear God, since you have not withheld your son, your only son, from Me" (Genesis 22:12). Abraham had passed the test. What was he to do now, though, with the altar? It would seem inappropriate to build an altar and walk away from it. Furthermore, he desired to worship God, who had just spared his son. As he contemplated what to do, a movement caught his eye. Looking up, he caught sight of a ram wedged in a nearby thicket. Carefully freeing the ram, he gladly offered it on the altar in place of his son.

At this point we might be tempted to focus on the fact that God had provided a substitute sacrifice, and skip over the important detail that it was a *ram*. How significant is this?

When God later gave instructions to Moses about sacrifices, He required that any animal offered must be without blemish. Although Abraham lived a long time before Moses, we have every reason to believe that he understood very well that God required perfection. Therefore, if God would have sent a lamb to Abraham on that day, it may have become injured in its struggle to extricate itself from the thicket. The ram, however, was caught by its horns. It could not get free and run away, and it would not have been wounded in the struggle. It was, therefore, a suitable sacrifice. Surely Abraham grasped the significance of this miracle. God had provided exactly what he needed.

After offering the ram as a sacrifice to God, Abraham decided to name the place where he had constructed the altar *Jehovah-Jireh* because "In the mount of the LORD it shall be provided" (Genesis 22:14). The Hebrew word *jireh* serves as the root for the word *roi* that we looked at previously. Essentially these words have the same meaning. Hagar called God *El-Roi* (the God who sees me), and Abraham named the mountaintop where he offered his sacrifice *Jehovah-Jireh* (God will see). As both Hagar and Abraham realized, God not only sees, but He provides.

One of the greatest men of faith that has ever lived is George Mueller. God used him to establish what can only be described as an orphanage empire in Bristol during the nineteenth century. Although the needs of caring for thousands of orphans were enormous, Mueller never once asked any person for help. He adamantly refused to even give an answer when asked about current needs. It was only when he published his annual *Narrative* that the public could observe how God had provided in the previous year.

In March of 1839, a man read Mueller's *Narrative* and was touched by his faith. As he read, he developed a special burden for his sister who owned an expensive jewelry collection, which included a diamond ring. In prayer, he begged God to show his materialistic sister the trivial nature of her collection. His prayer that she would lay her jewelry on the altar was answered, and she eventually donated it to Mueller's work. The contribution came at a time of extreme need, and the proceeds from the sale of the jewelry covered a week's expenses. Before Mueller sold the diamond ring, he carried it into his bedroom, and with it carved into the window pane the words *"Jehovah-Jireh."*[3] In the years to come, whenever he experienced deep poverty, he looked at those words and remembered that "the Lord will provide." He may not provide in ways that we can foresee, but He will provide nonetheless.

Worship God for His Provision

God does not simply "see" what is happening in our lives. He sees *and* provides. He saw Hagar's need and provided for her. He saw Abraham's need and provided for him. Furthermore, He does not have to scramble around trying to react to surprises. The Lord who sees knows in advance what to provide. As Abraham and Isaac were climbing up one side of the mountain, an innocent ram was meandering up the other. Coincidence? I don't think so. God was working it all out, moving everything into place before anyone else knew what would be needed. The future is just as clear to God as the past is to us. The needs you will have in the future are currently unknown to you, but you can rest assured that God is facilitating a plan to take care of you.

From time to time I see a sign that says "a failure to plan on your part does not constitute an emergency on mine." It's a good thing that God doesn't always feel that way about us. He knows what we will be up against in the future and He takes precautionary measures so the need is met at the right time.

When I was newly married, I purchased life insurance. While I hope it will never be needed, I know that it is possible. If I were no longer in the picture, my family would need a source of funding to be able to live. Therefore, I saw the possibility of a need and provided for it. That is exactly what the names *El-Roi* and *Jehovah-Jireh* signify. Long before we know about a need, God is taking care of it.

Many people understand Abraham's statement in this passage as a direct reference to the death of Jesus Christ, predicting that God would provide *Himself* as the lamb for the ultimate sacrifice. While I am not sure that Abraham had that in mind, the idea is accurate. This whole event takes place on the same mountain range upon which Jesus was crucified many centuries later. He did, in fact, see our need of salvation from sin and He provided the way for us to be set free.

Reflections on Chapter 6:

The *Provision* of His Name

1. How did Hagar move from simply hearing about God's existence to understanding that He was involved in her daily life?

2. How might Hagar have responded to God if He had seen her plight and ignored it?

3. How could Abraham be so sure that he and Isaac would both return from the mountain?

4. Why is it significant that Abraham found a ram to sacrifice instead of a lamb?

5. Although *Jehovah-Jireh* literally means "Jehovah sees," what does the name indicate about God?

6. In what ways has God provided for needs in your life before you knew you had them?

Chapter 7

The *Supremacy* of His Name

The LORD of hosts is with us; the God of Jacob is our refuge.
(Psalm 46:7)

Consider what it would be like to live in constant danger simply because you hold certain religious beliefs. Every time you dare to attend a church service, you fear that you will never come back. You find yourself hiding your Bible in a secret compartment so it will not be discovered. You refuse to let your children out of your sight because it is possible that they will not return. Although this scenario may seem foreign to twenty-first century Americans, it was commonplace in much of the world during the early sixteenth century. The greed and false teaching of the Roman Catholic Church prompted many to reject its claim to be the one true representative of God on the earth. Those who rebelled faced the wrath of not only the Church, but often of the political leaders who mandated conformation to their personal religious beliefs.

Among the most prominent rebels of this era was Martin Luther, a priest who became so fed up with the greed of the Church that he compiled a list of ninety-five reasons why the

Pope was mishandling the practice of selling indulgences. He carried his list to the Wittenberg church in 1517, and boldly nailed it to the door for the whole world to see. This courageous act, which garnered the attention of both his enemies and those sympathetic to his cause, became the spark that was fanned into the flame of the Protestant Reformation. The Reformation, however, became much more than a mere religious dispute. It proved to be an all-out war in which many lost their lives.

In 1529, Martin Luther composed a song describing his view of the Reformation. It is said that whenever he found himself in trouble, he would ask his associate to join him in singing the words of the song.[1] It described so well the mindset of the Reformers that it became known as the "Battle Hymn of the Reformation." We know it better as "A Mighty Fortress." The lyrics were originally written in German, but here are the first two verses as they have come down to us in English:

A mighty fortress is our God,
A bulwark never failing;
Our helper He amid the flood
Of mortal ills prevailing.
For still our ancient foe
Doth seek to work us woe;
His craft and power are great,
And armed with cruel hate,
On earth is not his equal.

Did we in our own strength confide,
Our striving would be losing,
Were not the right man on our side,
The man of God's own choosing.
Dost ask who that may be?

Christ Jesus, it is he;
Lord Sabaoth, his name,
From age to age the same,
And he must win the battle.

We often think of God as we need Him at the moment. When our lives are progressing smoothly, we think of Him as the One who provides blessings. When we sin, we tend to view Him in His role as a judge. When we are repentant, we consider His faithfulness to forgive. Martin Luther, in the throes of intense persecution wherein thousands of Christians were experiencing martyrdom for their faith, needed a companion who could fight. That is why he thought of God as Lord Sabaoth. But what does this title mean, and where did he get it?

Luther based his famous song on the forty-sixth chapter of Psalms. I would encourage you to open your Bible and read this chapter, trying to view it as Luther would have under his circumstances.

In verse seven of this passage, David wrote that "the LORD of hosts is with us." The term "LORD of hosts" in the Hebrew is *Jehovah-Sabaoth*. You will recognize *Jehovah* from our previous discussion, but what does *sabaoth* mean?

Jehovah-Sabaoth – The Lord of Armies

The word *sabaoth*, when used in the Scriptures, is most commonly translated as "hosts." It is a transliteration of the Hebrew word that sometimes describes heavenly bodies (Genesis 2:1), but usually is used in reference to armies, either of men (Genesis 26:26) or of God (Joshua 5:15). Referring to God in this manner indicates that He is not merely the commander of an obscure military unit, but that He has the charge of a vast army.

Jehovah-Sabaoth holds ultimate authority. David realized this when he engaged in his notorious face-to-face altercation with Goliath, the most dreaded enemy of the Israelites. Looking his larger-than-life enemy directly in the eyes, he warned, "You come to me with a sword, with a spear, and with a javelin. But I come to you in the name of the LORD of hosts . . ." (1 Samuel 17:45). David knew that an attempt to find strength in any man would be vain. He went straight to the top.

Have you ever labored for hours on the phone with an incompetent low-level answering service employee who could not get anything done for you? Maybe you were trying to get to the bottom of a discrepancy on your electric bill or credit card, but all your questions were answered with, "I'm sorry, sir, I can't do that." After you have finally had enough, what do you do? You demand to talk to a supervisor. Granted, you may be transferred to the employee in the adjoining cubicle, but you're willing to take that chance. You just want a conversation with someone who has the ability to take care of your problem. That is what David was doing. How much higher can you go than God? He is the LORD of hosts, *Jehovah-Sabaoth*. He is in charge. He has all of creation at His beck and call.

The majesty of this name is further revealed in Isaiah's recounting of the vision wherein he was transported to the throne room of God. The seraphim that he observed gathered around the throne took it upon themselves to constantly proclaim, "Holy, holy, holy is the LORD of hosts; the whole earth is full of His glory!" (Isaiah 6:3). Although many prefer to reject the authority of God and even deny His existence, the whole earth is permeated by His glory. Not to mention Heaven itself!

The fact that the Old Testament prophets were partial to the name *Jehovah-Sabaoth* shows that it fit with their motif of God being one who requires justice. Isaiah, who repeatedly referred to

God in this manner, warned that "the day of the LORD of hosts shall be upon every one that is proud and lofty, and upon every one that is lifted up; and he shall be brought low" (Isaiah 2:12 KJV). It may seem for a while as if the wicked will get away with their evil, but they will be held accountable in the end.

In keeping with the military connotation of this name, consider a city that is under siege by a massive army. Comparing numbers, the leaders of the city may be forced to surrender, acknowledging the impossibility of organizing a successful defense. You may have heard of Masada, which was a fortress built on the top of a steep mountain in Israel. Approximately a thousand Jews retreated to this well-fortified stronghold when the Romans moved in for the final destruction of Israel. In 74 AD, Masada fell, but when the Romans reached the top, they found nothing but corpses. The Jews had committed mass suicide and burned their own fort. They knew that it would be impossible to resist a Roman attack, and they refused to allow the Romans to receive credit for the slaughter. They understood that in a battle, the side with the greatest power wins. That is the same reason it is futile to attempt to struggle against God. He is *Jehovah-Sabaoth*. We may get away with some things for a while, but He will have the final word.

Knowing the power of *Jehovah-Sabaoth*, we may think of Him as a hateful power in the sky to whom we must fearfully submit. However, rather than visualizing God as an evil warden who has all the forces of Heaven zeroed in on us with the intention of sadistically zapping us over the smallest misstep, think instead of having all of those forces on our side! The LORD of hosts has the means whereby He can help us when we need it.

If you were a terrorist hiding in a desert, and observed the United States Marines surrounding your hideout, would you be scared? Of course you would. Marines are highly trained and exceptionally devoted to the security of their country. Sworn enemies of the United States should shake in their boots when confronted by these brave men and women. However, now imagine that you are stranded in your car amid the raging waters of a flash flood, expecting to be swept to your death at any moment. The appearance of the National Guard would not bring you fear, but relief. What is the difference? The difference is whose side you have taken. You fear the military if you are an enemy, but welcome it when you are in trouble. Is it any different with God? We have no need to fear *Jehovah-Sabaoth* when we are obedient.

Have you ever been introduced to a couple named Elkanah and Hannah? You may know them better as the parents of the prophet Samuel. Hannah, after years of failed attempts to become pregnant, traveled to the Temple in Jerusalem to spend some time in distressed prayer to God. She so strongly desired to remove the stigma of barrenness that she made a pledge to God. If she were allowed to have a son, she would give him back to God. Recognizing the power of the God who could fulfill her request, she chose to call Him by the name *Jehovah-Sabaoth* (1 Samuel 1:11). If anyone could allow her to conceive, it would be the LORD of hosts.

How did God respond to this request? Did He rebuke her for squandering His valuable time with what might be considered a minor irritation for one who is managing the universe? Absolutely not. The LORD of hosts, *Jehovah-Sabaoth*, heard her prayer, saw her faith, and granted her request.

The fact that God is *Jehovah-Sabaoth* has great personal application for us. Between the Old and New Testaments is a time period that we generally call the four hundred silent years. Malachi, an Old Testament prophet, gave God's message to the Israelites, and then no one heard directly from God for about four hundred years. Then all of a sudden, out of the blue, John the Baptist arrived on the scene boisterously proclaiming to everyone within earshot that the Messiah was soon to appear. Why would God be silent for four centuries only to set things spinning so quickly that the events of the whole New Testament took place in a span of only about a hundred years? Unfortunately, we are not told. However, if someone stopped talking to me for four hundred years, I would mentally replay our last conversation to find out if there was something I had done wrong. That's what Malachi's job was—to explain what was wrong. The first chapter of his book presents God's view of the wickedness of Israel in no uncertain terms. What is bizarre about it is that He rebuked them for doing what He told them to do in the first place!

Let me clarify myself. The Israelites were doing *what* they were supposed to do, but not *how* they were supposed to be doing it. Let's listen in a little to find out what message from God Malachi was to relay.

A son honors his father, and a servant his master. If then I am the Father, where is My honor? And if I am a Master, where is My reverence? Says the LORD of hosts to you priests who despise My name. Yet you say, "In what way have we despised Your name?"
(Malachi 1:6)

Good question. God informed the Israelites that they did not even honor Him as they would honor a father or a master. The priests (and the people) would puzzle over this rebuke. *What are you talking about? We do what God wants. We bring our sacrifices to the Temple like we are supposed to. What's the problem?*

The problem was that at best, they offered half-hearted service to God. Sure, they lugged their sacrifices up to the Temple, but instead of choosing the best of the flock, they had picked out the blind, the lame, and the sick to give to God. This was entirely unacceptable. After all, they would never treat honorable men so disgracefully.

> *And when you offer the blind as a sacrifice, is it not evil?*
> *And when you offer the lame and sick, is it not evil? Offer it*
> *then to your governor! Would he be pleased with you? Would*
> *he accept you favorably?" says the LORD of hosts.*
> (Malachi 1:8)

We are no better than the Israelites who first heard Malachi's rant. They offered God things that they would never get away with offering to those who held honor among them.

Consider what would happen if you gave the same amount of energy to your career as you gave in your service to God. Would your boss keep you around? If others repeatedly have to cover for you when you don't show up, or your manager has to constantly prod you to do your work, how long will it be before you find yourself scanning the help wanted ads?

While your employer is worthy of your best service because he signs your paycheck, God is worthy of your best because He is the "Lord of hosts." *Jehovah-Sabaoth.* Malachi continued with the words of God:

> *"My name shall be great among the Gentiles; in every place incense*
> *shall be offered to My name, and a pure offering; for My name*
> *shall be great among the nations," says the LORD of hosts.*
> *(Malachi 1:11)*

God will get His glory, and it would be in the best interest of the Israelites to glorify Him by offering Him their best.

I know that you probably do not drag a lamb to church on

Sunday morning for your pastor to sacrifice on the communion table. If you do, I recommend seriously re-thinking your theology. However, you offer a host of other things to God—your time, your skills, your money, and so much more. The question is, do you offer Him the absolute best, or just enough to get by? If you teach a Sunday school class or lead a small group discussion, do you prepare like you were going to be giving a sales pitch to an affluent client? If you clean the church building, do you make it shine as if the president of the United States had planned a visit? If you are in the rotation to sing a special or play in the band, do you perform as if a talent scout might be in the service?

I am not suggesting that everything we do must be flawless. There are some areas in my life where I just do not have that ability. Regardless of how hard I try, flaws will still be evident. However, there are other areas in which I can reach perfection if I am willing to put a little heart into it. Each person's best will be different. *Jehovah-Sabaoth*, the supreme, majestic God, is worthy of *my* absolute best.

The fact that God possesses power far beyond that of man is evidenced in His name *Jehovah-Sabaoth*. However, as if to impress upon us the truth of His supremacy, the Old Testament prophets provide us with a second name that bears similar meaning.

El-Gibbor – The Mighty God

God had given His prophet Jeremiah a bizarre command. He was to go out and buy a piece of property. Normally this would not have been a strange request, but under the circumstances it was quite peculiar. Nebuchadnezzar, the king of Babylon, was beating down the walls of Jerusalem, poised to bring the land of Israel under his dominion. His plan, which ultimately succeeded, was to relocate the inhabitants of Jerusalem to Babylon, leaving the land basically desolate. What good would a parcel of land do for Jeremiah? As it turns out, the purchase was designed to be an object lesson. God commanded Jeremiah to place the deed to the land in a piece of pottery and bury it. In doing so, he showed the Israelites that although they would be taken into captivity, and their land would be ransacked, God would one day bring them back to their homeland. He had promised the land to the descendents of Abraham, and although they receive temporary punishment for their sins, nothing could permanently halt His plans. As Jeremiah contemplated the power of God that would bring about such a miraculous event, he prayed:

> *You show lovingkindness to thousands, and repay the iniquity of the fathers into the bosom of their children after them—the Great, the Mighty God, whose name is the LORD of hosts.*
> (Jeremiah 32:18)

You may recognize the phrase "the LORD of hosts," which we have just seen is translated from *Jehovah-Sabaoth*. Jeremiah inserted another name, however, which is translated as Mighty God. This name is a combination of *El* (the supreme being) and *gibbor* (pronounced with a hard "g"), which implies the power of a warrior. Like *Jehovah-Sabaoth*, it is a military term.

Nebuchadnezzar, the capable leader of the most powerful nation on the earth at the time, was no match for God. The commander of the greatest of human militaries is rendered impotent when confronted with the armies of Jehovah. At the time of Nebuchadnezzar's conquest, it seemed that no force could bring the Babylonian Empire to its knees. God, however, was working out a plan. No king can stand against *El-Gibbor*, the mighty God.

Throughout history, there have been numerous occasions

when God's people have experienced oppression by the armies of the world. Beyond the battles against Israel that we see in the Old Testament, the Jews continue to encounter hatred into the modern era. The Holocaust serves as a prime example, but the hatred extends even to today. Although most of the nations of the world succumb to pressure and reject Israel, God is still with this great nation. Furthermore, non-Jewish Christians around the world frequently are oppressed by secular governments. Most North Americans do not understand the extent to which the church is being persecuted around the world.

Is there any hope for Christians who persist in worshiping Jesus Christ even though their lives are at risk? There is if one considers that *El-Gibbor,* the mighty God, will one day issue the command of final destruction for the ungodly kingdoms of men. Those who have experienced persecution and martyrdom for the cause of Christ, ones "of whom the world was not worthy" (Hebrews 11:38), will observe the mighty power of God displayed in an undeniable fashion. As followers of Jesus Christ, we are on the winning side, regardless of how bleak the outlook seems today.

Around Christmas we often discuss this recognizable passage about the coming Messiah, Jesus:

> *For unto us a Child is born, unto us a son is given; and the government will be upon His shoulder. And his name will be called Wonderful, Counselor, Mighty God, Everlasting Father, Prince of Peace.*
>
> (Isaiah 9:6)

"Mighty God," used as a description of Jesus Christ, is *El-Gibbor.* Although Jesus is indeed the loving and compassionate Savior of the world, He is one day going to act in His capacity of captain of the hosts of God. With incontestable supremacy, he will lead the armies of Heaven in the final vanquishing of the Devil.

Jehovah-Nissi – The Lord our Banner

Once again, we have come to a name that was applied to an altar instead of directly to God. In this case, Israel was engaged in a battle with its perennial enemy, the Amalekites. As the fighting commenced, God instructed Moses to stand at the top of a hill overlooking the battleground, clutching his rod above his head. As long as he held it up, Israel prevailed in the battle. However, as soon as he surrendered to his aching muscles and lowered his arms to rest, the tide turned, and the Amalekites began to prevail. Moses, of course, was unable to hold his rod above his head indefinitely. Noticing his predicament, his brother Aaron and a friend named Hur came to the rescue. They found a big rock and shoved it under Moses so he could sit down. Then Aaron squatted on one side of him while Hur settled in on the other. They hoisted his tired arms on their respective shoulders and together they watched as God gave Israel the victory. At the conclusion of the battle, Moses built an altar on the spot and named it *Jehovah-Nissi* (Exodus 17:15).

We already know that the name Jehovah points to the existence of God. *Nissi* refers to a banner or a standard.[2] Think about the pictures you have seen of the Revolutionary War. A flag-bearer marches along a dusty road followed by a string of disheveled and weary soldiers. Regardless of the danger they face, the fatigue they experience, or how much they long to be home, they follow their flag into battle. It is their ensign. It is their standard. As long as the flag is still flying, everything is "ok."

Most Americans have heard the story of Francis Scott Key. Temporarily held hostage on a British ship in 1814 while bargaining for the release of a fellow American, he watched helplessly as the British mercilessly attacked Fort McHenry. For twenty-five hours the bombardment continued, until it suddenly ceased the morning of September 14th. As the sun began to rise,

Key peered through the haze to see if the fort had fallen. To his amazement and exultation, the flag continued to wave above the fortress. Fort McHenry had tenaciously refused to surrender, and the British had finally decided to abandon the attack. The emotion Key experienced at the sight of his beloved flag inspired him to compose a poem that would later become known as "The Star-Spangled Banner," the national anthem of the United States of America. The flag was a symbol of strength. As long as it continued to wave, the battle was not lost.

When Moses named his altar "The LORD our Banner," he demonstrated his understanding that Israel could only win battles under the blessing of Jehovah. It was not Moses who won the battle against the Amalekites, and neither was it the two unsung heroes, Aaron and Hur. Nor was it Joshua, who bravely led the ground forces against the enemy. It was God whose power made all the difference.

Have you ever experienced a battle in your life? You may not have dodged bullets or shrapnel, and maybe your life has never been in danger. However, the battles we face as Christians are real. There is a spiritual war taking place all around us. We cannot see it, but we can know it is there. Our enemies do not drive tanks or carry automatic weapons because "we do not wrestle against flesh and blood, but against principalities, against powers, against the rulers of the darkness of this age, against spiritual hosts of wickedness in heavenly places" (Ephesians 6:12). If you decide to go off on your own to tackle your enemy, you will suffer devastating defeat. Instead, fight under the ensign of *Jehovah-Nissi*, the LORD our banner.

Worship God for His Supremacy

There are many ways for us to think of God. We may imagine Him sometimes as a judge and at other times as a comforter. We may focus only on one aspect of His character to the exclusion of the others. However, a balanced approach is necessary. The military names of God afford us a more comprehensive picture of who He is. While His supreme strength requires us to recognize Him as the judge to whom we must submit, His power also makes it possible for us to bring our requests to Him in faith, knowing that He has the ability to provide what we need.

Reflections on Chapter 7:

The *Supremacy* of His Name

1. Why did Martin Luther view God as Lord Sabaoth?

2. How should the name *Jehovah-Sabaoth* bring us both fear and comfort?

3. What does the name *El-Gibbor* mean for the persecuted church and for you personally?

4. What is the connection between *El-Gibbor* and Jesus Christ?

5. Why did Moses call his altar "The LORD our Banner?"

6. How should knowledge of the supremacy of God affect your daily life?

Chapter 8

The *Healing* of His Name

I am the LORD who heals you.

(Exodus 15:26)

Healing is a topic that seems to be on everyone's mind today. The healthcare industry has grown enormously because people will pay almost anything to experience relief from their physical ailments. Addiction recovery has also become a booming business as people seek freedom from the bondage of alcohol and recreational drugs. We also face a host of emotional and mental difficulties that require specialized help.

Where do we turn in the midst of all this unrest? We can consult with doctors, counselors, and therapists, but never discover the healing that we need. We are then left to deal silently with the question that is on the minds of people across the world: *Is there anyone who has the answers for all the pain and suffering that we are forced to endure? Is there any hope for relief?*

In a previous chapter, we discussed *El-Olam*, the name of God that indicates His ability to be present with us because he is everlasting. Now we will consider a name that shows a very practical result of His presence—that He offers healing.

Jehovah-Rapha – The God who Heals

In the fifteenth chapter of Exodus, Israel had just emerged from a prolonged bout of slavery in Egypt. The exultation they experienced in their newly found freedom unfortunately came to a screeching halt rather quickly. The Egyptians had supplied them with all kinds of necessities in their hurry to rid themselves of these folks who had been instrumental in bringing the destruction of the plagues upon them. A very important necessity that they could not provide, though, was an endless supply of water. Therefore, after traveling a mere three days into the wilderness, the Israelites began to get thirsty. Imagine their joy when they finally spotted some water! The instant they saw it, "Chariots of Fire" began playing in the distance, life turned into slow motion, and a swarm of Israelites floated gracefully across the desert to be the first in line.

Whether they later named this place Marah (bitter) or if it was called by this name before they arrived, we do not know. However, it lived up to its name. The first person to arrive at the bank leaned over, took a big swig, and immediately gagged. The water was bitter and unfit to drink. Jubilation promptly turned to disappointment. Immediately the complaints began, as would be the custom for the next forty years. Moses, the innocent object of the criticism, consulted God about what to do. God directed him toward a certain tree that he was to cut down and throw into the water. When he did so, the bitter waters became sweet and the Israelites could drink to their hearts' content.

We do not know the location of Marah, and neither do we know what kind of tree it was that transformed the potability of the water, but that is irrelevant. The lesson that God wanted to teach the Israelites was clear. Let's hear it straight from His mouth.

If you diligently heed the voice of the LORD your God and do what
is right in His sight, give ear to His commandments and keep all
His statutes, I will put none of the diseases on you which I have
brought on the Egyptians. For I am the LORD who heals you.

(Exodus 15:26)

God treated this event as an object lesson. In a sense, He was saying, "See what I can do? If you can learn to obey me, you will not have to experience the difficult things that you have seen the Egyptians endure. The God who can heal water can also heal you." He then introduced a new name for Himself, one that appears only in this place: *Jehovah-Rapha. Rapha* means "heal."[1] Through the unveiling of this name, Jehovah revealed that He is the one who can provide healing. Not just for water, but for people as well.

While we often think of healing in connection with physical ailments, God's healing power is multi-faceted, extending beyond the physical into the emotional and spiritual realms. Let's take a quick look at each of these areas.

He has power over physical healing

It is unfortunate that when we think of "healing" we often envision a flamboyant evangelist sporting wild hair and holding massive crusades to which people flock, hoping to be cured of their physical maladies. While I tend to view these events with a high level of suspicion, I admit that the Bible is clear that God is able to heal physical illness.

The reason that we have to endure physical sickness is that sin has entered the world. However, the God who made us perfect in the first place holds absolute power over our health. After all, who is more able to fix something than the one who made it?

I once heard a story about an inventor who designed a very complex one-of-a-kind machine for an overseas company. After it had been in use for a while, it shut down and nothing the on-site technicians attempted would get it working again. Finally, the exasperated employees decided to place a call to the machine's inventor. He immediately booked a flight and was on the scene in two days. When he arrived at the location of the machine, he spent fifteen minutes investigating the internal mechanisms. Finally, he reached into his toolbox, pulled out a hammer, and forcefully struck the machine one time. Instantaneously, it whirred to life. The technicians were elated that the problem was so easily resolved, but their excitement turned to dismay when two weeks later they received a bill for five thousand dollars. Because that seemed like an enormous charge for one hammer strike, they sent a request back to the inventor to supply a breakdown of the charges. His response was simple and consisted of only two lines. At the top of the page was written "$5 for hitting the machine with a hammer." Under it they read "$4,995 for knowing where to hit it."

Although we put a lot of faith in physicians and scientists who have studied the makeup of the human body, God alone holds infinite knowledge about how it works. Therefore, we should not seek God merely as a last-ditch effort when we have no other answers. Why not first seek the advice of the inventor?

In the Bible we read the account of Asa, a king of Judah who started off his reign by serving God with his whole heart. However, by the time he came to the end of his life, he had replaced his trust in God with dependence on man. As he neared death, he developed a serious disease in his feet. Rather than asking God for healing, which he probably would have done early in his reign, he instead consulted only with his podiatrist. The sad commentary that "in his disease he did not seek the LORD, but the physicians" (2 Chronicles 16:12) reveals God's displeasure for this misplaced trust. Interestingly, the word "physicians" is translated from the Hebrew word *rapha* that is used in the compound name *Jehovah-Rapha*. Asa's downfall was that he sought for healing in the knowledge of men rather than the power of God. The physicians were *rapha*, or healers, but they could not heal this sickness.

Would God have cured Asa if he would have asked? We are not given an answer to this question, but his life definitely ends on a low note. The next verse states that he died in the fortieth year of his reign. Was God waiting to show Himself strong through this king who at one time had been so faithful? Possibly. But Asa failed.

Turning to the New Testament, we acquire further instructions about God's healing power and how to receive it.

Is anyone among you sick? Let him call for the elders of the church, and let them pray over him, anointing him with oil in the name of the Lord. And the prayer of faith will save the sick, and the Lord will raise him up. And if he has committed sins, he will be forgiven.

(James 5:14-15)

When we read that the prayer of faith will "save" the sick, we should not think of it in the same light as the salvation of our souls. The word "save" is a generic term that carries the idea of deliverance. Rather than providing eternal salvation through the prayers of others, what is taught here is that God will hear the prayers of the elders of the church on behalf of those who are sick. However, we cannot overlook James' statement that God will forgive the sins of the sick person if any have been committed. I believe that James is communicating the truth that sometimes sickness comes as a direct result of a specific sin. The person who is in this predicament and comes to the elders of the church realizes his sinfulness and humbly admits it. In that case God sees both his heart and the prayers of faith offered by the elders, and responds with both physical and spiritual deliverance. He heals the sickness and forgives the sin.

It is important to understand that although God often provides healing in response to prayer, we cannot expect that God will always heal whenever we ask. If that were the case, no one would ever die! The point of this passage is not that God is a cosmic vending machine that will bestow our desires upon us whenever we press the correct button or speak the magic words. Rather, we can be assured that He has the power to answer our prayers, and the later statement that "the effective, fervent prayer of a righteous man avails much" (James 5:16) should encourage us to persist in prayer.

He has power over emotional healing

Maybe the healing you need is emotional rather than physical. Can God help with that, too? David surely thought so. In his distress he cried out, "Have mercy on me, O LORD, for I am weak: O LORD, heal me, for my bones are vexed" (Psalm 6:2 KJV). To be vexed is to be agitated. Have you ever felt that way? Maybe you have a name for it, such as anxiety or depression. Whatever you call it, David experienced it. For him, it was emotional or spiritual rather than physical. However, he had assurance that in Jehovah he would find the strength to persevere. On another occasion, as he dedicated his newly constructed house, he recalled that for years he had been forced to live in caves as he dodged the wrath of King Saul. He also considered the many wars he had undertaken against his enemies. Gazing with wonder at his beautiful house and recollecting all the blessings he had received since those tumultuous days of the past, he praised God by recalling, "I cried unto You, and You healed me" (Psalm 30:2). This was not physical healing, but emotional. Many of David's psalms were born out of severe difficulties in his life, but God helped him through them all.

He has the power to heal the effects of sin

While sin is clearly described in the Bible as a choice and we must not think of it as a disease, it does have consequences, and these consequences need healing. In the third chapter of Jeremiah, we find that God held Israel accountable for her harlotry because she had abandoned Him and went to serve other gods. Yet He pleaded, "Return, you backsliding children, and I will heal your backslidings" (Jeremiah 3:22). Their choices had left them in a broken-down condition that needed to be repaired.

Sin is destructive. It leaves devastating wounds, which David understood well. After he sinned he pleaded, "LORD, be merciful to me; heal my soul; for I have sinned against You" (Psalm 41:4). Although David was clearly a man of God, he failed often and experienced the repercussions of his decisions. He needed God to heal (*rapha*) him after these painful experiences.

He punishes in mercy

When we consider the reasons that we should worship God, punishment may not be the first thing to come to our minds. After all, we worship God for good things, right? He is holy, He is righteous, He is eternal, He is powerful, and He provides. But can we honestly say that we desire to worship Him because He punishes us? Who likes to be punished?

I don't know about you, but when I administer punishment to my children, they never gaze upon me with appreciative eyes and say, "Thank you for loving me enough to take away something I really enjoy so I can learn obedience." Unless your progeny has far surpassed mine in spirituality, it probably has not happened at your house, either. So, what makes punishment so great? It is that God uses it to teach His people obedience, which allows them to fulfill their purpose in life.

Have you ever seen a K-9 officer with his dog? The dog is obviously very contented. He frolics like a playful child, seemingly oblivious to the cares of life. However, as he is playing, he continuously looks to his handler for instructions. He never seems upset that he has been denied the opportunity to roam the streets freely for the rest of his life, desperately scouring the garbage cans for scraps to fill his empty stomach. His precision training allows him to enjoy a permanent home, good food, and a purpose.

That is what God does for His people with punishment and discipline. If we were free to roam and do our own thing, we could never fulfill God's purpose for our lives. He has to train us to be what He wants us to be, and that is sometimes a difficult process.

In the nineteenth chapter of Isaiah we have the privilege of listening in on the prophet's prediction about Egypt, which had been historically viewed as an extremely powerful nation. In the end, this polytheistic nation will come to know and worship God (verse 21). The pathway, however, will not be easy. God will first strike Egypt, then heal (*rapha*) her (verse 22). He will allow a cruel tyrant to overtake the land. The Nile River, which makes Egyptian life possible, will become dry. The Egyptians will be riddled with fear, and, believe it or not, a good portion of their fear will be served up compliments of the tiny nation of Judah. All of this will prompt the Egyptians to realize that Jehovah, the God of Judah and Israel, is the one true God. Like so many others, Egypt will not come to this realization from simply hearing it told. Instead, the nation will have to experience great difficulty while God thunders down on its inhabitants the truth of His existence. He has to smite before He can heal.

The prophet Hosea also realized that God often works in this way. He pleaded for his fellow Israelites to return to the worship of Jehovah because "He has torn, but He will heal us; he has stricken, but He will bind us up" (Hosea 6:1). What kind of a God would He be if He allowed us to persist in our sin without retribution? To borrow an old slogan from the United States Army, we would never be able to "be all that we can be" without harsh discipline and precision training. We should be thankful that God punishes us, because it allows us to heal from the effects of our sin and we can be all that we were made to be.

Worship God for His Healing

Do you need healing? Maybe it's physical healing that you require. Maybe it's emotional. Or possibly you are dealing with God's punishment because of your sin as God attempts to heal you from your affliction of disobedience. When you need healing, where do you go? God has provided us with a medical industry that has discovered much about His design in nature, and these findings can help us immensely. But where does God fit into your plans when you need healing? Is He your last resort or your first resort? Always remember that He is *Jehovah-Rapha*, the LORD who heals. Take your physical, emotional, and spiritual needs to Jehovah, who alone holds the power to cure all of your diseases.

Reflections on Chapter 8:

The *Healing* of His Name

1. What lesson was God teaching the Israelites when He healed the waters at Marah?

2. King Asa sought for help from physicians. Does this mean that it is wrong to go to doctors for help? If so, why? If not, what was Asa's real mistake?

3. What is the point of James' reference to praying and healing in James 5:14-15?

4. What can be learned from David's prayer to God in Psalms 6:2?

5. What personal benefit to do we receive from God's punishment?

6. What lessons can we learn from God's predicted punishment on both Egypt (as prophesied by Isaiah) and Israel (as prophesied by Hosea)?

Chapter 9

The *Purity* of His Name

For He made Him who knew no sin to be sin for us, that
we might become the righteousness of God in Him.

(II Corinthians 5:21)

I spent the year of 1997 as a short-term missionary in Russia. If you have ever lived for a lengthy amount of time in a foreign country, you can relate to the fact that I discovered rather quickly that much of life was different there than in the United States. Several months into my stay, I broke a tooth, which required a dental appointment. After making some inquiries, I found out that most of the dentists work in the school buildings, so one afternoon I made an appointment. The dentist seemed to do a great job, and I sure couldn't beat the price. The next time I needed dental work done, I went back to her, this time in the morning. During the course of conversation through my interpreter, the dentist mentioned that I was fortunate to have scheduled my appointment in the morning. She proudly informed me that she sterilizes the tools at night, which means they are clean for the early patients. I couldn't help remembering that my first visit was in the afternoon. I wonder how many mouths those tools had been in before I arrived.

When I sit drooling in the dentist chair, trying to find a way to non-verbally answer the doc's incessant questions, I want everything that enters my mouth to be dedicated to me. I like to watch the dental assistant rip open the package of clean tools and place them on a sterilized cloth. I suspect that you would probably agree with me. If I am going to be terrorized by those instruments of torture, the least I can expect is that they are dedicated for my own use.

God desires the same thing. He not only *wants* but *requires* absolute purity and dedication from those He uses as tools in His service. That is what we are shown through the names we will discuss in this chapter.

Jehovah-Tsidkenu – The Lord our Righteousness

If you have studied the history of Israel, you may remember that after the death of Solomon, the kingdom of Israel was divided into two nations: Israel in the north and Judah in the south. In 722 BC, as a result of unrelenting idolatry, God allowed Assyria to destroy Israel. Judah, however, continued to exist, as its inhabitants frequently made attempts to turn back to God. However, by 586 BC, God was fed up with Judah's repeated return to idolatry. He allowed the Babylonians under King Nebuchadnezzar to ransack Jerusalem. They took most of its inhabitants into captivity, leaving the land desolate. In the meantime, God sent the prophet Jeremiah to those in Judah to inform them that their sin was the reason for the devastation. In the twenty-third chapter of his book, he placed the fault squarely on the leadership of Judah.

"Woe to the shepherds who destroy and scatter the sheep of My pasture!" says the LORD. *Therefore thus says the* LORD *God of Israel against the shepherds who feed My people: "You have scattered*

*My flock, driven them away, and not attended to them. Behold, I
will attend to you for the evil of your doings," says the* LORD.

(Jeremiah 23:1-2)

The shepherds (or leaders) of Judah had failed in their duty.
Not only had they neglected to protect their flock, but they
had actively led it astray! As a result, God promised to inflict
punishment on the whole nation. The Israelites would soon find
themselves scattered around the world, enslaved by their enemies.

Jeremiah's message, however, is not one of absolute doom.
Immediately following the disastrous prophecy came good news.
God would "gather the remnant of My flock out of all countries
where I have driven them . . . and they shall be fruitful and
increase" (Jeremiah 23:3). God would free them from captivity
and permit them to return to their own land where they would live
without fear. Eventually God would "raise to David a Branch of
righteousness; a King shall reign and prosper" (Jeremiah 23:5). In
the days of this king, Israel would finally be able to live in safety.

Who is this king? He is identified as "the LORD our
Righteousness" (Jeremiah 23:6). In Hebrew it appears as *Jehovah-
Tsidkenu.* The Hebrew word *tsidkenu* means "righteousness."[1]
The significance of this name is only understood if we fully
comprehend the predicament of the people of Judah. Therefore,
we should continue looking at Jeremiah's prophecy.

"Therefore, behold, the days are coming," says the LORD, *"that
they shall no longer say, 'As the* LORD *lives who brought up the
children of Israel from the land of Egypt,' but, 'As the* LORD
*lives who brought up and led the descendants of the house of
Israel from the north country and from all the countries where I
had driven them.' And they shall dwell in their own land."*

(Jeremiah 23:7-8)

The Old Testament indicates that the Israelites often referred to God as the one who brought them up out of slavery in Egypt. That event was the major turning point in their history as a nation. However, since then, they had been scattered around the world, just as God promised would happen if they rebelled against Him. As we have already seen, Israel and Judah were destroyed by the Assyrians and Babylonians. Although many of the captives later returned to their land, they were unable to revive their status as a powerful nation. Finally, in 70 AD, the Romans destroyed Jerusalem. The land of Israel sat basically desolate until the end of the nineteenth century, when "something" caused the Jews to begin to migrate back to their homeland. In 1948, the miraculous occurred when Israel once again proclaimed herself a nation and became a significant player on the world scene.

So there's your short history lesson. We took time to look at it because today we sit at a vantage point that allows us to more thoroughly understand Jeremiah's prophecy than any other time in history. Many Jews today experience an inexplicable draw toward the land of Israel, even against the wishes of a majority of the world. This proves that something supernatural is taking place. God is placing within His chosen people an inner drive to return to their homeland, the physical land of Israel.

You may wonder, however, what the righteousness of God has to do with bringing the Jews back to their land. Remember the reason that He drove them into other countries in the first place? It was because they had rebelled against Him. After they come back into their land (as we see taking place today), they will eventually realize that their troubles were a result of their own sin, and that God can only accept them when He places undeserved righteousness upon them. He will take an unworthy nation and make it worthy.

Now that we understand why the name "the LORD our

Righteousness" is significant for the Jews, what does it mean for those of us who are classified as Gentiles? It is important because although God is not restoring a geographical homeland for us, He accepts us as unworthy people. Like the Israelites, we have been unrighteous. This poses a serious problem for us because since God is righteous, He cannot recognize anything good in us. When measured against the standard of perfection, we "fall short of the glory of God" (Romans 3:23).

As a child, I always felt a sense of pity for "city slickers." They were the kids whose parents forced them to live in concrete jungles where the only way they could get dirty was by putting their hands in a sanitary sandbox that was hardly big enough to serve as a kitty litter. I distinctly remember, as all well-adjusted humans should, manufacturing mud pies in the back yard. After a long day of toiling in the "factory," we could not understand why Mom refused to allow us into the house. Muttering something under her breath about a freshly mopped floor, she would force us get cleaned up, at least to the point where we were almost recognizable. Only then could we take our seats at the table. You may have experienced similar circumstances, and probably do the same with your children. When they come in from playing outside, what is the first thing you tell them to do? "Take off your shoes!" If they are really messy, you might strip off their clothes at the door and douse them with the garden hose. When questioned, your explanation is simple. "I just cleaned the house and you're not going to mess it up!" No one wants all that filth in a clean house.

Now consider the glory of God, which is ultimate perfection. God despises the filth of sin. It is diametrically opposed to who He is. Can you see how that poses a major problem for us? Just as we may be prohibited from entering a house with muddy shoes on our feet, we are prohibited from entering Heaven with the filth of sin clinging to us. Sin and righteousness do not mix.

The good news is that while His righteousness poses a problem, His righteousness also provides the solution. Our righteousness that was lost through sin needs to be restored. Unfortunately, we have become so utterly depraved that even our best efforts cannot restore it. It is impossible for us to purge enough sin out of our lives to be labeled again as righteous.

Imagine that you have before you a glass of water and a gallon of automotive antifreeze. Antifreeze has the capacity to serve as both a blessing and a curse. It extends the life of your car by preventing the water in the radiator from freezing, but it will terminate your life quickly if you ingest it. You never want to leave antifreeze in an open container because pets and other animals will be attracted to its sweet but lethal taste. Knowing that, would you pour some antifreeze into your glass of water and drink it? Of course not. As soon as antifreeze is introduced into the glass, the glass is considered contaminated. Now let's say that you pour out the antifreeze, rinse the glass several times, then fill it up again with fresh water. Would you drink it now? I don't know about you, but I would not touch it. As far as I am concerned, the glass has been permanently tainted. I will never knowingly drink out of it, regardless of how often it is washed.

In God's eyes, we are like that glass. Sin has utterly contaminated us. No amount of adding good things into our lives can make us pure again. Just as you would look for a new glass if you were thirsty, you need to be made a new person. That is the beauty of Paul's statement that "if anyone is in Christ, he is a new creation" (2 Corinthians 5:17). We are not rinsed or reformed. We are recreated. A few verses later we see how this happens. God has made Jesus, who "knew no sin to be sin for us, that we might become the righteousness of God in Him" (2 Corinthians 5:21). We had sin and Christ had righteousness. However, Christ took our sin on Himself (and the Father forgave it at the cross) and put

His righteousness on us, making us completely new, without the taint of sin. While we are still living in the flesh, we will struggle with sin, but on the inside we have been made new.

Unfortunately, we cannot take this to mean that *every* person has become righteous. This process is applied only to select people: those who believe. To the Romans, Paul pointed out that it is not through works that God's righteousness is applied to someone, but "his *faith* is accounted for righteousness" (Romans 4:5, italics mine). God does not ask for reformation or adherence to a specific religion. He does not require us to conform to a long list of rules or traditions. If that were the case, we would prove to be dismal failures. Instead, He asks for faith. Through faith in Christ, God exchanges our sin for His righteousness. The next name of God that we will discuss illustrates this further.

Jehovah-Maccaddeshem – The Lord our Sanctifier

Possibly the first thing you noticed about this name of God is that it is quite a mouthful, especially in a culture that prefers names like Bob, Jim, or Sally. Fortunately, it is more important to know what this name means than to be able to remember or pronounce it. To understand it, then, let's revisit the occasion when God instituted the Sabbath as a time of rest for Israel.

Speak also to the children of Israel, saying: 'Surely My Sabbaths you shall keep, for it is a sign between Me and you throughout your generations, that you may know that I am the LORD who sanctifies you.'
(Exodus 31:13)

The seventh day of the week was to be considered a day of rest for the Israelites. It was a day that God had set apart for a specific purpose. To illustrate this, God labeled Himself as "the

Lord who sanctifies you," or *Jehovah-Maccaddeshem*, as it appears in Hebrew. *Maccaddeshem* describes the process of sanctifying or consecrating something, which basically means to set it apart as holy. The Israelites were to set the Sabbath day apart from all the other days of the week. It was special. It was to be considered as a sign between God and the Israelites that God had set them apart from all other nations. They were His chosen people. As He rested from creation on the seventh day, they should follow His example and do the same. Each Sabbath, as they kicked back and relaxed, they would remember that out of all the nations in the world, God had chosen Israel as His favorite.

This "setting apart" of the Israelites helps us to understand why God gave them the Law. As His specially chosen people, He desired their purity. After all, they had been charged with the responsibility of sharing the glory of the righteous God with the whole world.

Sanctification, however, is not solely for Israelites. God set that nation apart to be his chosen people, but He also sets Christians apart from others in the world. Jude noted this when he addressed his book "to those who are called, sanctified by God the Father" (Jude 1:1). This sanctification, or setting apart, of believers is possible because of the new covenant by which "we have been sanctified through the offering of the body of Jesus Christ once for all" (Hebrews 10:10). Although Israel and the Church exist as two distinct entities, God has consecrated each to bring deserved glory to Himself. Israel was to show His power to the world, and the Church is to show the way of salvation through Jesus Christ.

The question that we should have is this: "Am I living as a consecrated person?" The Israelites lived out their consecration, in part, by observation of the Sabbath. But what about us? Should it not be obvious in our daily lives that we have been set apart by

God? Paul announced that the will of God is for every Christian to "know how to possess his own vessel in sanctification and honor" (1 Thessalonians 4:4). It is the will of God that we *act* like we *are!* We are set apart by God for the purpose of glorifying Him, so we should act like it. After all, Jesus "gave Himself for us, that he might redeem us from every lawless deed and purify for Himself His own special people, zealous for good works" (Titus 2:14).

Worship God for His Purity

Have you ever accepted the righteousness of God for yourself? Remember that you cannot manufacture your own righteousness. That is what religion attempts to do, but fails. God does not ask us to be religious. He asks us to have faith. You cannot do enough to change yourself from unrighteous to righteous. God has to do it Himself. His standard is too high for you.

This book is about worshiping God. Remember, to worship is to attribute worth or to give honor to someone. If God went through all that He did to allow the righteousness of Christ to be placed on us, would it not be dishonoring to reject it?

My two oldest boys have birthdays that are six days apart. One year I decided to give them a joint present, so I spent numerous hours in the basement making a "kiddie" picnic table for them. The day of the big presentation finally arrived. With great pride I hoisted my creation on my shoulder and carried it up the stairs. Stepping out onto the deck, I anticipated the excitement that would be shown for my skill and labor of love. The boys, however, did not seem to appreciate its magnificence as much as I did. They took one look at it and went back to playing with their toys. I couldn't believe it. I had labored diligently for them, and yet they failed to express their eternal, undying commitment and love for me. Where were the echoes of praises that should have been sung in my name?

Maybe we treat the gift of God in a similarly ungrateful fashion. He did much more than screw a few 2X4s together to make a table. He paid a hefty price to convert a bunch of worthless rebels into something capable of entering into His presence. Should He not, then, be worthy of our most sincere worship?

You can worship God best by accepting His gift by faith, allowing Him to place His righteousness on you. He offers you the gift of salvation, and it honors Him for you to receive it with appreciation. After that, you can worship Him by living out the truth of consecration. You have been set apart to serve Him, so to borrow a phrase from Nike, just do it!

Reflections on Chapter 9:

The *Purity* of His Name

1. What is the significance of the name *Jehovah-Tsidkenu* for the Israelites?

2. Why does God require righteousness to be placed on those who would desire to enter His presence?

3. What is the process whereby we can get the righteousness of Jesus applied to us?

4. How does the observance of the Sabbath day illustrate the idea of sanctification and purity?

5. We have been set apart by God to show His glory to the world. Can you think of ways in which you can fulfill this responsibility?

6. What is the best way to show worship to God?

Chapter 10

The *Discipline* of His Name

Now no chastening seems to be joyful for the present, but
painful; nevertheless, afterward it yields the peaceable fruit
of righteousness to those who have been trained by it.

(Hebrews 12:11)

If you could do one thing with the guarantee that you would
never suffer the consequences for doing it, what would it be? If
you are a devout rule-follower, the fact that I would dare ask such
a question causes you distress. Others (you know who you are)
can immediately pinpoint three or four activities that you would
love to do, *if only* there were no consequences.

Once when I was a child, I thought I observed my younger
sister get by with telling my parents "no," so I decided to test the
waters myself. After all, would it not be great to live by my own
rules, without any consequences? Needless to say, that was the
one and only time I attempted such a foolish thing. I immediately
received an unmistakable reminder that rebellion was not an
option in our house.

We all live under some form of regulations, which may be
enforced by an employer, the government, or even church leaders.

While we do not always enjoy the inhibition caused by such rules, most of them are for our own good. Therefore, when our disobedience produces chastisement that makes us think twice the next time, it is beneficial to us in the long run. In the previous chapter we discovered the purity of God, revealed in His names *Jehovah-Tsidkenu* (The LORD our Righteousness) and *Jehovah-Maccaddeshem* (The LORD our Sanctifier). We have received the righteousness of Jesus Christ, authorizing us to enter into the presence of the holy God. One day our glorified bodies will permit us to physically enter His presence. In the meantime, however, our righteousness should be modeled in our lifestyle. Unfortunately, we often do a good job of masking it. To help us live up to the reality of who we are, God has given commands in His Word. We must obey them or face the consequences.

If you have children, you know that commands are worthless without consequences. Too many parents are guilty of screaming at their kids (for the fifth time), "If you do that one more time, I'm going to ground you for life!" Or, "This is the last time I'm going to tell you!" A child that is used to such empty threats will rarely obey.

Our human nature prompts us to do whatever we want when there is no punishment for disobedience. Therefore, God provides an ultimatum when He issues commands. He even calls Himself by two names that show that He is serious about discipline.

Jehovah-Nakah – The Lord who Strikes

We previously discussed Jeremiah, the prophet whom God sent to the inhabitants of Judah as the Babylonians, under Nebuchadnezzar, were whisking them away into captivity. Now we will consider his fellow prophet Ezekiel, who also prophesied during the Babylonian captivity.

The idea that God permitted His chosen people to be enslaved to a pagan nation may be disconcerting to you. If God is omnipotent and loves His people, why would He allow them to be destroyed by a nation as ungodly as Babylon? Furthermore, in the book of Daniel we find Nebuchadnezzar described as an egotistical tyrant, especially early in his reign. Why would God allow him to defeat Israel? It may shock you even more to realize that not only did God *allow* it; He *orchestrated* it. How could He do such a thing?

Ezekiel answered this question when he relayed God's message that "My eye will not spare, nor will I have pity; I will repay you according to your ways, and your abominations will be in your midst. Then you shall know that I am the LORD who strikes" (Ezekiel 7:9). The phrase "the LORD who strikes" is a combination of Jehovah (I Am) and *nakah*, which refers to striking (or hitting) something. Usually when *nakah* appears in the Bible, it describes killing another person, such as in battle. When used of Jehovah, it certainly does not depict the soft and cuddly version of God that many Christians envision today. God was making it clear that the Babylonians were not ultimately responsible for the destruction of Jerusalem. He was merely using Babylon as a pawn to do His will. He did not only allow it, but He caused it to happen because of the sin of the Israelites.

God's response to the sin of Judah teaches us an important lesson and provides us with a balanced and accurate view of God. Whereas we prefer to think of God as a God of love, we need to remember that true love holds people responsible. Fathers and mothers who refuse to hold a child accountable for her actions will one day grieve, trying to determine where they failed as parents. They may wonder why their child is lazy, can't hold a job, and refuses to listen to authority. The simple reason is that the child has not been taught responsibility or respect. God has called us to be parents of our children, not just friends. As our kids mature, we can communicate with them increasingly on a peer-to-peer basis, but until the day comes that they venture out on their own, they are under our authority. Children may not understand why we supervise their friendships, prohibit certain shows on television, or refuse to allow them to play computer games all day. They may complain and make us feel like we have failed miserably in our parental roles. A good parent, however, will place restrictions on a child, because the discipline will ultimately allow her to develop into a productive adult.

We would do well to remember the comparison between earthly parents and God as found in Hebrews, where it is pointed out that "for whom the Lord loves He chastens, and scourges every son whom He receives" (Hebrews 12:6). If you endure punishment for your sin, it just may be a good indication that you are truly a child of God. Furthermore, "if you endure chastening, God deals with you as with sons; for what son is there whom a father does not chasten?" (Hebrews 12:6-7). That is a good question. What kind of father does not punish his children when they need it? In the same way, when we are guilty of disobedience toward God, we bring punishment on ourselves.

God does not punish us because He gets sadistic enjoyment out of watching us suffer. The punishment we receive for our sins is part of the overall discipline that we receive from God. He does not inflict punishment in uncontrolled anger. Instead, He provides training that will allow His children to serve Him more capably. The Psalmist recognized this when he said, "Before I was afflicted I went astray: but now I keep Your word" (Psalm 119:67). What did he mean by "afflicted?" A few verses later he indicated that these afflictions were the ones pronounced on him by God during a time of chastisement. "I know, O LORD, that your judgments are right, and that in faithfulness You have afflicted me" (Psalm 119:75).

The idea of God using Babylon to punish Judah may seem unfair. We can accept the fact that God had to punish Judah, but why would He bless a pagan nation by allowing it to reap the rewards of defeating His people? Surely the Babylonians thought, "We are successful, so we must be doing something right!" What they did not realize, however, was that success does not prove that one is right. God used the Babylonians for a while, but their day of judgment finally arrived. Although God used them in the destruction of Judah, He made plans to punish them for their involvement in it. This is what we will see as we return to Jeremiah's prophecies.

Jehovah-El-Gemulah – Lord God of Recompense

Although God used Babylon to punish His people for their sins, He planned to return the punishment on this wicked empire. Jeremiah foretold of the destruction that the aggressors would experience:

> *Because the plunderer comes against her, against Babylon, and*
> *her mighty men are taken. Every one of their bows is broken; for*
> *the LORD is the God of recompense, He will surely repay.*
> (Jeremiah 51:56)

The term "LORD God of recompense" is comprised of Jehovah (I Am), *El* (the Supreme Being), and *gemulah*, which means, of course, "recompense."[1] Through this prophecy, God revealed that He will punish His enemies.

To recompense is to give someone what is deserved. Although

the Babylonians were used by God to do His will, they deserved punishment for their aggression against God's people. God could not allow this sin to go unpunished. This fact is stressed by Jeremiah's words that God "will surely repay." A literal translation from the Hebrew would be that God will "repay repay." The word is doubled to show emphasis. We cannot miss this point. No question about it, God will pay back what the Babylonians deserve.

Hold on a minute. Once again, that does not seem fair! How is it that God would prompt the Babylonians to destroy Judah, then punish them for doing it? We need to understand that the Babylonians were worthy of punishment well before this whole event transpired. God was simply using them to fulfill His purposes before He meted out their punishment. This is very similar to what He did to the Canaanites when He originally brought the Israelites into the Promised Land. He commanded His people to destroy every one of them, but it was not because He is unfair or plays favorites. The Canaanites well deserved to be destroyed. God had made this clear.

> *It is not because of your righteousness or the uprightness of your heart that you go in to possess their land, but because of the wickedness of these nations that the LORD your God drives them out from before you, and that He may fulfill the word which the LORD swore to your fathers, to Abraham, Isaac, and Jacob.*
> (Deuteronomy 9:5)

It was the sin of the Canaanites that prompted God to send destruction on them through the Israelites. Not only did the stench of their sin rise to heaven, but God knew very well that if these pagans were allowed to remain in the land, the Israelites would fall prey to their influence and begin to worship their false gods.

The unfortunate truth is that this very thing came to pass. Not all of the Canaanites were obliterated, and the ones that remained influenced the Israelites to involve themselves in idolatry. God would punish the Babylonians not only for the destruction of Judah, but because of their pagan lifestyle. This is what God promised through the prophet Jeremiah. How could they be sure, however, that God would do as He had promised? Well, He had a track record. After all, the last group of people who dared to fight against the Israelites had suffered a similar fate. To see this, let's backtrack more than 130 years to the destruction of the northern kingdom of Israel.

Assyria had taken the northern kingdom of Israel captive in 722 BC, well before the destruction of Judah in 586 BC (by the Babylonians). During the time between these two events, the prophet Nahum wrote about the coming destruction of Nineveh, the capital of Assyria.

> *God is jealous, and the LORD avenges;*
> *The LORD avenges and is furious.*
> *The LORD will take vengeance on His adversaries,*
> *And He reserves wrath for His enemies;*
>
> (Nahum 1:2)

Although God had used Nineveh to inflict punishment on His people, Nineveh, because of her wickedness, was still His enemy and would be punished herself. If you were an inhabitant of Israel who had been taken captive, however, you might have wondered what was taking God so long to return the punishment to His enemies. Nahum answers this question also.

> *The LORD is slow to anger and great in power,*
> *And will not at all acquit the wicked.*

The LORD has His way
In the whirlwind and in the storm,
And the clouds are the dust of His feet.

(Nahum 1:3)

God often does not work quite as fast as we think He should, because He is slow to anger. However, we can be assured that He will not acquit the wicked. He will never turn a blind eye to wickedness and proclaim the guilty to be innocent. The people of Nineveh were wicked and would be punished.

Nahum proceeded then to describe the power that God would unleash on those who dared stand against Him:

He rebukes the sea and makes it dry,
And dries up all the rivers.
Bashan and Carmel wither,
And the flower of Lebanon wilts.

The mountains quake before Him,
The hills melt,
And the earth heaves at His presence,
Yes, the world and all who dwell in it.

Who can stand before His indignation?
And who can endure the fierceness of His anger?
His fury is poured out like fire,
And the rocks are thrown down by Him.

The LORD is good,
A stronghold in the day of trouble;
And He knows those who trust in Him.

But with an overflowing flood
He will make an utter end of its place,
And darkness will pursue His enemies.

(Nahum 1:4-8)

God had used Assyria to punish Israel, and He would soon use Babylon to punish Judah. However, both of these empires would later be judged for their involvement.

Israel and Judah endured much suffering because of their sins, and we should expect the same. Although we live in a different era, we still have the same God who loathes sin and holds His people accountable. However, we may find that even when we try to live in obedience, we still have enemies. Paul noted to Timothy that "all who desire to live godly in Christ Jesus will suffer persecution" (2 Timothy 3:12). Righteous living does not provide us with a "get out of suffering free" card. We can expect tribulation in our lives because we live in a world that is bursting with ungodliness. When it comes, we may be tempted to take matters into our own hands and give our "enemies" what they deserve. However, it is God's job to do the judging. We are not to take revenge into our own hands. Retribution is God's business.

Repay no one evil for evil. Have regard for good things in the sight of all men. If it is possible, as much as depends on you, live peaceably with all men. Beloved, do not avenge yourselves, but rather give place to wrath; for it is written, "Vengeance is Mine, I will repay," says the Lord.
(Romans 12:17-19)

Our natural response is to give our enemies what they deserve. When someone hurts us, we crave to return the favor.

When we hear a derogatory rumor that is being spread about us, we want to embark on a witch hunt to find out who is behind it. God commands us, though, to be patient. Let Him take care of the retribution. After all, is He not the one before whom the mountains quake? Is He not the one whose fury is poured out like fire? Let Him prescribe retribution when it is necessary! As for ourselves, we should just be thankful that He has imparted mercy to us and refrained from giving us what we deserve.

Worship God for His Discipline

How do you view God? It is very easy to develop an unbalanced understanding of His character. On one hand, we can single out His love and forgiveness. If this is all we consider, we defang God and make Him nothing more than a huggable teddy bear whose sole purpose is to cuddle with us when we feel bad. On the other hand, we can consider Him to be a vengeful ogre who destroys anything and everything in His path. The truth about God, however, is balanced. He is love, but true love does not allow sins to go unpunished. As we submit to His loving discipline, we will be enabled to become what we were created to be, and for this we should worship Him.

> *Now no chastening seems to be joyful for the present, but*
> *painful; nevertheless, afterward it yields the peaceable fruit*
> *of righteousness to those who have been trained by it.*
> (Hebrews 12:11)

Reflections on Chapter 10:

The *Discipline* of His Name

1. Why would God allow and even orchestrate the captivity of His chosen people in Babylon?

2. How does punishment indicate love?

3. What is the difference between discipline and chastisement?

4. How do you explain the fact that God punished the Babylonians after He had used them to accomplish His will?

5. Why does God not punish evil as quickly as we think He should? What does this mean personally for you?

6. What should be our response when our "enemies" fight against us?

7. How should we balance the love of God with His hatred of sin?

Chapter 11

The *Care* of His Name

The LORD is my shepherd; I shall not want.

(Psalm 23:1)

It was a sad day in the Hammond house. A few months earlier we had acquired a bunny, a cute little fur ball with one ear that stood straight up and one that hung limp. The kids played with Cinnamon every chance they could get. One morning, however, they came running to me with terror in their eyes and informed me that Cinnamon was not in his cage. Sure enough, the chicken wire was torn and no bunny was to be found. We searched in all the neighbors' yards to no avail. Then I caught a glimpse of the one thing that I did not want to see. Lying in the middle of the street was a rabbit. Our forensics expertise (thanks to CSI) allowed us to determine that a dog or some other large animal had destroyed the cage, setting our beloved pet free. He only made it to the street before he was either mauled to death or hit by a car.

I remember clearly the pain on the faces of my children, who were quite young at the time. Together we dug a grave, and as I lowered Cinnamon into it, Caleb gently reached out to him for one final touch. My heart broke. How do you help children understand the concept of death?

Death is a part of life. As we grow older, we find that more and more of our friends are crossing to the other side. During these difficult times, we often look into the Bible for something that will provide comfort. The most common passage that fulfills this need is the twenty-third chapter of Psalms. In this psalm, God is depicted as a shepherd. Although in the previous chapter we discussed that God disciplines His people, we also learned that God does not punish out of spite. He lovingly cares for us in the same way that a shepherd cares for his sheep. All the truths that we have learned about God are necessary, but in times of grief what helps most is to realize that there is someone who cares. It is comforting to know that we have a shepherd who is constantly looking out for us.

Jehovah-Ra'ah – The Lord our Shepherd

The opening phrase of Psalm 23, "The LORD is my shepherd," is comprised of Jehovah (I Am) and ra-ah (shepherd). David, who wrote this psalm, possessed an intimate knowledge of sheep, having "shepherd" listed on his own résumé. As he compared God's relationship with His people to the work of a shepherd, he noted many similarities. Therefore, to understand how God cares for His people, it would be fitting for us to look at some of the key ideas in this beloved chapter.

A shepherd provides for the needs of his sheep

When I was a child, I was slightly confused when I read "The LORD is my shepherd; I shall not want." It seemed to me that David was saying he would not want God as his shepherd. As I got older I realized that David was contemplating the fact that if God was his shepherd, what else did he need? A shepherd's job is to make sure his sheep do not lack any necessities. We do not know if David penned this psalm while he was still a shepherd or if he wrote it years later from his palace, fondly reminiscing about his days watching sheep on the hillside. In either case, he knew that as a shepherd, he had carefully watched his sheep to determine what they needed. Never did his sheep have to worry about where the next meal was coming from or where they would find their next drink of water. He had taken care of all of it for them.

With Jehovah as our shepherd, we also will never lack what we need. He provides us with green pastures and still waters (verse 2), which are the basic necessities for sheep. He also prepares a "table before me in the presence of my enemies" (verse 5). I suspect David was not thinking of a solid oak table with matching handcrafted chairs. Even in our culture when we speak of a "table," we do not always refer to the table itself, but the fellowship that takes place around it. The table is a symbol of bounty. The great thing about the table that God provides is that He has prepared it. He knows what we need and He has it ready, often well in advance. When we are faced with a need, He does not have to turn His cupboards upside down like Old Mother Hubbard, frantically searching for some way to provide for us. He anticipates our needs and has the table already prepared.

Before I was married, my circle of friends included two young ladies who were a few years older than me and still unmarried at the time. These girls, while waiting on their respective knights in shining armor to swoop into their lives and sweep them off their feet, shared an apartment. One of them invited me to come to supper one evening, and when I arrived, her roommate was home alone. No table was prepared and it was obvious the roommate was not expecting me. We engaged in small talk for a while, then I left without indicating the real purpose of my visit. A short time later I received a phone call from a very apologetic friend after she arrived home and found out I had been there. She had completely forgotten about the invitation! You can be sure this will never happen with God. He is already making preparations, and will not be caught by surprise when you show up with a pressing need.

In addition to the fact that the table is prepared ahead of time, it is important to note that the table exists "in the presence of my enemies." What is significant here is that there is no promise that all of our enemies will be removed and life will be a breeze. If that were the case, there would be no need of a shepherd!

The knowledge that the shepherd leads us to green pastures and still waters and also provides us a table in the presence of our enemies shows us that we are not rid of brown fields, dry wells, and dangerous enemies. If life were a utopia, we would have no need of a shepherd to provide for us and keep us safe. I do not have to convince you that we have great needs. I do want to assure you, though, that in the midst of these needs, we have a Shepherd who is both able and willing to take care of them.

A shepherd provides comfort for his sheep

While we have been given no promise that God will provide everything we want, we can be assured that, as the Shepherd, He does provide comfort. In Psalm 23:3, David says that God "restores my soul." To restore something means to bring it back to a previous condition. If you are like most normal people I have met, sometimes you feel gloomy. The ominous clouds of depression may darken your horizon. Possibly you have endured a heartbreaking experience, and you want to get back to the place where life is enjoyable. I have good news for you. He can restore your soul. He can get it back to where it should be.

One of the most difficult situations with which we will be confronted is death, whether we are faced with our own mortality or the loss of a loved one. David noted that as the Shepherd, God is with us even while journeying "through the valley of the shadow of death" (Psalm 23:4). Even though we as Christians know what is on the other side, there is still the fear of facing something that extreme for the first time. I have often heard people speak of "dying grace," wherein God provided an inexplicable peace when they knew that their time on earth was short. I have also seen it firsthand. Just as sheep can take comfort in the presence of the shepherd as they traverse through the dangerous mountain passages on their path to lush pastures, we can be assured of God's presence when death is our companion on the journey through life.

A shepherd provides protection for his sheep

"Your rod and Your staff, they comfort me" (Psalm 23:4). Wait a minute. The rod and staff sound like instruments of brutality. How are they supposed to offer me comfort?

In his book *A Shepherd Looks at Psalm 23*,[1] Phillip Keller discusses the purpose of the rod and staff. He describes the rod as a short stick that the shepherd used for protection. As a young boy, a shepherd-in-training would select a perfect piece of wood and handcraft his own rod. He would spend many hours practicing until he could skillfully throw it at anything that threatened the sheep. One almost pities the unsuspecting beast that ventured too close to the flock only to be sent yelping into the wilderness after being struck by precisely aimed airborne rod.

A shepherd provides guidance for his sheep

In His role as a Shepherd, God "leads me in the paths of righteousness" (Psalm 23:3). The paths of righteousness are sometimes difficult for people to find, because we naturally want to go the wrong way. We need guidance.

In this wonderful age of modern technology, many of us are blessed with the use of a GPS in our car. We call ours "Mandy" (my wife secretly enjoys watching me take directions from a woman). When we don't know where to go, we ask Mandy. Although at times she gets confused and we end up lost in some place like downtown Chicago, most often she has kept us on the right path. No longer do we have to scribble down directions when we want to travel. We just punch in the address and away we go. It doesn't matter that we have never been there before.

How many of us have previously attained to righteousness? No one. Therefore, we need guidance from God, the only one who knows the way. Sometimes this guidance comes in the form of chastisement, which is one of the purposes of the rod and staff (Psalm 23:5). Phillip Keller indicates that the rod and staff, beyond their role in protection, were also used for discipline of the sheep.[2] Should an adventurous sheep decide to wander away from the flock into dangerous territory, the shepherd would throw the rod in its direction, forcing the animal back to safety. The staff, the other primary tool of the shepherd, was longer than the rod and usually had a hook on one end. With the staff, the shepherd was able to keep his flock together. He could easily reach out and pull a wandering sheep back to himself or nudge a newborn lamb back to its mother.

It is easy to see how these tools would provide comfort to the sheep. Although the inquisitive lamb may not enjoy being yanked back into line when he is hot on the trail of some interesting diversion, he can rest assured that the staff restores him to a place of safety. As long as he is close to the shepherd, no harm will come to him. The shepherd does not use his rod and staff out of hatred or anger toward the sheep, but because he desires to guide an ignorant or rebellious animal into the right path. As the true Shepherd, God does not punish us out of anger, but because He desires to guide us into doing what is right. After all, like sheep, we can be too independently minded.

My youngest son has always possessed a rather independent streak. When he was barely big enough to walk, he got loose and immediately sprinted (or rather waddled) down the main aisle at a grocery store, never looking back. I trailed him for a while at a distance, but he did not know nor did he care. I finally had to snatch him mid-stride and carry him back where he didn't want to be, because that was best for him. Although he much preferred to go his own direction, as his loving father I imposed my own will on him. The end result was his safety. Our Shepherd does the same thing for us.

Worship God for His Care

While God the Father (Jehovah) is compared to a shepherd, Jesus refers to Himself in the same way.

> *I am the good shepherd. The good shepherd gives His life for the sheep. But a hireling, he who is not the shepherd, one who does not own the sheep, sees the wolf coming and leaves the sheep and flees; and the wolf catches the sheep and scatters them.*
> (John 10:11-12)

A good shepherd will risk his life for his sheep because he loves them and feels a strong sense of responsibility toward them.

He refuses to leave them defenseless when faced with danger. Jesus, as the Good Shepherd, did just that. When faced with death, He did not back down. He literally gave His life so we could live. Does that not indicate to us that He is worthy of worship?

As we consider both Jehovah and Jesus (two members of the Trinity) as being our shepherd, we need to remember that the promise given to us is that we "shall not want" and not that "we shall not want anything." There are many things that we desire, and the Shepherd allows us to acquire some of them. However, we are not guaranteed to have such things. Rather, the promise is that we will have what we *need*. Specifically, our needs are guidance and protection, which lead to comfort. The Shepherd does not remove the brown fields, empty wells, and dangerous enemies from our lives. Rather, He provides us with what we need in the midst of all of these difficulties. When you have needs, why don't you bring them to the Shepherd who alone has the ability to take care of them?

Reflections on Chapter 11:

The *Care* of His Name

1. What did David mean when he said that God provides a table?

2. Why is it significant that God provides us a table in the presence of our enemies?

3. How does God restore our soul? Have you ever come to a place where you needed this?

4. What roles do the rod and staff play in discipline and protection? How do they provide comfort to the sheep?

5. How did Jesus prove His dedication as the Good Shepherd?

6. With God as our Shepherd, we "shall not want." What exactly does this mean, and how do we reconcile it with the fact that we may have unfulfilled desires?

Chapter 12

The *Peace* of His Name

*Therefore, having been justified by faith, we have peace
with God through our Lord Jesus Christ.*

(Romans 5:1)

I do not know who is reading these pages and where you are located. I don't even know what year you are reading this book. It is possible that someone may find a copy of this work a hundred years after its publication date and know nothing about me other than what I have shared already. However, there is something I know about you. I know that the next time you pick up a newspaper or access the news on your favorite electronic device, you will find reports of famine, wars, and crime. Two nations may be battling over a disputed oil field, a terrorist attack may have just taken place, or the grocery store on the corner has been robbed...again. How do I know that these things are happening in your time and place? It's very simple. I understand man. It does not take long living in this world to sense that we are living amidst utter chaos. Some people deduce that all of this mayhem proves that there is no God. After all, if a loving and omnipotent Being does exist, why doesn't He step up and put an end to all of this pandemonium?

You may remember from our previous chapter that God refers to Himself as a shepherd. You may also recall that a shepherd does not remove the brown fields, empty water holes, and enemies from the world. Rather, he keeps his sheep safe in the midst of these perils. God has never promised that life would be easy or calm. However, in the midst of all the chaos and turbulence in the world, God provides us with the possibility of peace. This is the lesson of another important name.

In the sixth chapter of Judges, we read that the Midianites so greatly oppressed Israel that the Israelites deserted their homes and hid out in caves for fear of their lives. The Midianites took advantage of this opportunity and destroyed all of the abandoned Israelite crops and animals they could find. During the confusion, a relatively unknown farmer named Gideon sneaked out to his winepress to thresh wheat. He hoped that in this secret location he could slip under the enemy's radar and complete his harvest. While he nervously went about his business, the sudden appearance of a man he did not recognize startled him. Who could this be? A member of the ruthless Midianite army, perhaps? Imagine Gideon's shock when the stranger addressed him as a "mighty man of valor." I envision Gideon glancing around to see who else was standing there. I'm sure he didn't feel much like a man of valor, clandestinely sneaking out of town just so he could do a little work on his farm. Although he correctly surmised that this visitor must be an angel from God, his response does not seem overly friendly. Basically, Gideon's question was this: "Where is God? He brought our forefathers up out of Egypt only to allow us to be destroyed by the Midianites. Did He not do miraculous things for our ancestors? He gave them peace by setting them free from slavery in Egypt, but *what about now?*"

Gideon said to Him, "O my lord, if the LORD is with us, why then has all this happened to us? And where are all His miracles which our fathers told us about, saying, 'Did not the LORD bring us up from Egypt?' But now the LORD has forsaken us and delivered us into the hands of the Midianites."

(Judges 6:13)

Through the mysterious messenger, God gave Gideon a reply that he was not expecting. Instead of answering his questions, He informed Gideon that he had been selected to bear the responsibility of setting Israel free from the Midianites.

Gideon, as would be expected, entertained some doubts about this proposition. He was not a great warrior with a military pedigree. He was nothing more than an insignificant farmer who hid from the enemy like a coward. This couldn't be right. Someone was mistaken here. So, he asked for some kind of sign.

Before we criticize Gideon for his lack of faith, is it possible that we might have done the same thing? Imagine one day you are outside doing some lawn work and a stranger approaches you. He tells you that God has selected you to usurp control of the United States Armed Forces and proceed to defeat our nation's greatest enemy. Would you not seek some kind of evidence that he knew what he was talking about? Let's cut Gideon some slack. He needed some proof that this messenger was indeed from God.

Sometime during the course of the conversation, Gideon went inside and put together a meal for his visitor. When it was ready, he brought it out and placed it on a rock (apparently there was no picnic table at the winepress). However, instead of reaching for his fork, the angel touched the rock with his staff and immediately fire came up out of it and consumed the whole meal (Judges 6:21). As surprising as that would have been, more shocking was the fact that the mysterious visitor vanished along with the food. That was all that Gideon needed. He fully realized that he had indeed come face to face with an angel.

How would you have felt after an ordeal like that? Gideon, of course, was terrified. However, God spoke to him and said, "Peace be with you; do not fear, you shall not die" (Judges 6:23). When he heard those words, he did what so many others in the Bible did after having a conversation with God. He built an altar and gave it a name.

> *Then Gideon built an altar there unto the LORD, and called it Jehovahshalom: unto this day it is yet in Ophrah of the Abiezrites.*
>
> (Judges 6:24 KJV)

Jehovah-Shalom – The Lord our Peace

Gideon named his altar *Jehovah-Shalom*. You already know that Jehovah means "I am." *Shalom* is one of the most well-known Hebrew words, meaning "peace."[1] Why would Gideon combine these two words to form a name for his altar? I suspect that he had two reasons in mind. First, God had provided him with personal peace. When he realized that he had been in the presence of an angel, he had been terrified. However, God had comforted him with the words "peace be with you" (verse 23). The word "peace" is translated from, of course, *shalom*.

Not only had God provided Gideon with personal peace, but He had also promised to bring peace to the nation of Israel. This peace would not come through Gideon's power, but through Jehovah Himself. Gideon had not aspired to the position of army commander. In fact, the idea petrified him. However, he realized that God gave him the job and that peace for Israel would come through His power alone. As we take a further look at the adventures of Gideon, we will be able to see more clearly why the idea of peace was so prevalent in his mind.

Peace provides the strength to be obedient

The boldness that seized Gideon after his conference with the angel is remarkable. God had given him great peace about his newfound role in life. Before we go on, however, I must point out that peace is not always a sign from God that one is on the right track. Jonah, for example, while running from God, was peaceful enough to fall asleep in a ship that was being tossed by a terrible storm. I have had people tell me that they felt peace about following through with sins that are explicitly forbidden in the Bible. However, it is obvious that if God is in something, He can provide peace even though the storms are raging. That is the kind of peace that Gideon experienced.

Before Gideon went to bed the night after the incident at the winepress, his newfound peace would come in handy. God instructed him to do something that would certainly test his faith. He was to go into the town square, cut down the altar of Baal, and replace it with an altar to Jehovah. As recorded in verse twenty-five, he obeyed. As we would expect, this caused quite an uproar in town. Judging by the wrath of the local citizens, Gideon's action was more than a simple misdemeanor. It was probably akin to bulldozing the Washington Monument. However, knowing that he was acting out of obedience to God, Gideon had no problem with doing it. He experienced the kind of peace you can have when you know beyond a doubt you are doing what is right.

How did Gideon get such peace? Simply put, he had faith in what God said. After God proved that He was indeed the one speaking through the angel, Gideon was more than willing to obey. While a feeling of peace may not always be a reliable indicator that we are doing right, faith in God will always bring peace as we rest in the fact that He is in control.

Faith makes peace possible

I am sure you have noticed that we live in a world that is characterized by excessive anxiety. Our schedules are hectic, our bosses are demanding, and when we come home to take a break, we turn on the television and see that everyone is trying to kill everyone else. We might ask, "Where is peace in this chaotic world?" If we are searching for peace in the world system, we will be disappointed. Sin has absolutely corrupted mankind and rendered us unable to fulfill our purpose, which is to glorify God and have a relationship with Him. If we are not carrying out this purpose, we cannot be fulfilled.

To illustrate this, let's consider a fictitious person named Bob. After a long search, Bob is hired on at a certain company. He begins his career with great anticipation. He has plans to work hard and contribute to the business, eventually reaping the rewards of advancement. However, he soon realizes that he is given very little work to do and often finds himself fighting boredom. Although Bob may temporarily enjoy drawing a paycheck for doing nothing, he will soon begin to lack self-worth. Having few responsibilities, he cannot live up to his potential, which triggers internal anxiety. Eventually Bob will probably start looking for other employment.

While we often consider stress as the result of overwork, "underwork" can present the same symptoms. Man was designed to contribute to life, and when he cannot do so, he will experience stress. On a larger scale, that is the problem with man. Because of sin, we cannot do what we were designed to do.

The 1877 novel *Black Beauty* relates the story of a horse that experienced a dreadful life. Although a few of his numerous owners were kind, the majority treated him cruelly. Black Beauty was refused the ability to do what he was made to do—lope gallantly through the open fields, mane blowing in the wind, showing off his magnificent physique. Instead, for the greater part of his life he dragged carts through the crowded and dingy streets of London, slowly dying the death of one who has no purpose. In the same way, man is frustrated because, having no peace with God, he is unable to fulfill his purpose. He cannot do what he was created to do. He takes his feelings of discontent out in frustration on others, initiating wars and various types of crime. Nations fight against nations for a variety of reasons. Husbands and wives battle against each other. Church members squabble over insignificant preferences. It makes you want to stand up, grab a bullhorn, and at the top of your lungs scream, "PEACE!"

When the panel of judges asks a beauty contestant what she desires most in life, she customarily tosses her long hair, smiles into the camera, and delivers the answer everyone already knows she will give. *World peace.* Sure, that sounds great. But is it possible? After all, this earth has been around for thousands of years and we sure don't seem to be getting any closer to peace.

The only way for peace to become a reality is for man to be able to do what he was made to do. He needs to find some way to make peace with God.

How can we acquire this peace? It just so happens that we are given the exact recipe.

Therefore, having been justified by faith, we have peace with God through our Lord Jesus Christ.

(Romans 5:1)

Peace with God comes through faith in Jesus Christ. Faith justifies us, which means that God no longer holds our sin against us, making us acceptable to fellowship with Him. Although peace seems to be out of reach for most of humanity, it is possible. God will accept those who come to Him by faith.

There is therefore now no condemnation to those who are in Christ Jesus, who do not walk according to the flesh, but according to the Spirit.
(Romans 8:1)

Those who come to God by faith in Jesus are "in Christ." The Father accepts all those who are in Christ just as He accepts His own Son. In His eyes, we are no longer worthy of condemnation, but acceptance. That is the only way we can have true peace!

Worship God for His Peace

As we come to this point in our study, I hope that you have a better understanding of who God is. You know that He is the eternal, self-existent God. He is powerful and almighty. He provides for His people. He is supreme over all creation, yet present with us. He has the power to heal, and He is pure. He has the authority to discipline and He guides His people to safety. But what good is it to comprehend all of this if we do not have peace with Him? Instead of finding comfort in the almighty power and presence of God, we should be shaking with fear. He has infinite power, but He is not on our side.

When you attend a basketball game and out onto the floor trots a seven-foot center with muscles rippling under his tank top, how do you feel? That depends on whose side he is on, right? If he is wearing the uniform of your team, you feel a sense of comfort. However, if he is sporting the colors of the opposing team, you may feel some uneasiness. All that power will be fighting against you. How much more should you fear the omnipotent God when you are not on His side?

You can end your fears today by finding peace with God through faith in His words. He promised that if you believe in His Son Jesus Christ, you will have peace beyond what anyone can understand. Then all the characteristics of God that we have studied will produce comfort rather than fear. That is the theme of the final chapter of this book. You will not want to miss it!

Reflections on Chapter 12:

The *Peace* of His Name

1. Why did Gideon name his altar *Jehovah-Shalom?*

2. Is a feeling of peace a reliable indicator that we are doing what God wants us to do?

3. How did the peace Gideon felt influence his actions of obedience?

4. Why does man not have peace and how does it affect his actions?

5. How can peace be attained?

Chapter 13

The *Salvation* of His Name

*That at the name of Jesus every knee should bow, of those in heaven, and
of those on earth, and of those under the earth, and that every tongue
should confess that Jesus Christ is Lord, to the glory of God the Father.*

(Philippians 2:10-11)

In this book we have looked at many names that reflect on the
character of God. His three primary names are *Elohim*, *Yahweh*
(Jehovah), and *Adonai*. These indicate that He truly exists, that
He holds supreme authority, and that He is in ultimate control
of all. *El-Shaddai* and *El-Elyon* reveal His incredible power, and
El-Roi and *Jehovah-Jireh* tell us that He sees our needs and provides
for us. His supremacy is indicated in *Jehovah-Sabaoth*, *El-Gibbor*,
and *Jehovah-Nissi*. We have been comforted with the fact that
He is present in our lives as revealed in *El-Olam* and *Jehovah-
Shammah*. His healing power is shown in *Jehovah-Rapha*. *Jehovah-
Tsidkenu* and *Jehovah-Maccaddeshem* allow us a glimpse into His
purity. His purity requires Him to punish and discipline us, as
evidenced in His names *Jehovah-Nakah* and *Jehovah-El-Gemulah*.
The punishment we receive is a consequence of His care for us,

as noted in *Jehovah-Ra'ah*. Finally, we discovered the peace that He gives as exemplified by Gideon naming his altar *Jehovah-Shalom*.

All of these names, whether attributed to God, a city, or an altar, present reasons why we should worship God. We have considered many of His characteristics and how He interacted with people whose stories we read in the Bible. But how do we know that God *still* takes an interest in us? After all, most of what we have looked at comes from the Old Testament, which was written thousands of years ago. Does He still care? For example, Moses named his altar *Jehovah-Jireh*, which means that God sees. Does God see all people throughout all time or was this a singular event? Is it possible that we have merely observed some things He did just once and conjured up a false idea of who He is?

David used the name *Jehovah-Sabaoth* (Lord of Hosts) when fighting Goliath. Does God always enjoy this kind of superiority or was this an anomaly? Have we been guilty of taking one thing He said about Himself and pretending that it always fits Him? David also said, "The LORD is my shepherd" (*Jehovah-Ra-ah*). Sure, David thought so, but is He still the shepherd who guides, protects, and feeds His people in the twenty-first century?

People can say anything they want about themselves. But as is often said, "the proof is in the pudding." Talk is cheap. We read over and over in the Old Testament what God did for His people. But what about now? Has he done anything to prove to *us* who He is?

It just so happens that the apostle John must have considered the possibility that this question would arise, as he answered it all the way back in the first century AD. "In this the love of God was manifested toward us, that God has sent His only begotten Son into the world" (1 John 4:9). Lest there be any doubt that

God is still just as interested in us as He was in Moses, Abraham, and David, He proved His interminable love by sending His Son.

Every year on both Memorial Day and Veterans' Day, citizens of the United States come together to honor those who have left their homes and families to fight in order that they could acquire freedom and protect our nation. We also recognize those who have watched their sons and daughters go off to war with no assurance that they would ever return. Is there any greater sacrifice to prove that we love our country? We can proudly wave a flag at a parade and wax eloquent about our patriotism, but would we be willing to put our lives on the line to verify it? God proved who He was by making the ultimate sacrifice of sending His Son into a corrupt world to give His life on behalf of sinful man. Therefore, it is fitting that we end our study of the names of God by looking at the name of the Son of God, Jesus Christ.

While we often refer to Jesus as "Jesus Christ," the word "Christ" simply means "anointed"[1] and designates Jesus as the one chosen by God to save mankind. It is a title rather than a name. Jesus, on the other hand, is the name specifically chosen for him by God. This was the name that the angel Gabriel instructed both Mary (Luke 1:31) and Joseph (Matthew 1:21) to give to their miraculous child who would soon be born. The name Jesus comes from *Iesous*, which is the Greek form of the Hebrew name *Yehoshua*. In English, the name comes to us as *Joshua*, and means "Jehovah is salvation."

You might think it strange if someone in the United States named their child "Jesus," but if your name is Joshua, you can be proud that you have the same name as Jesus! Consider the Old Testament Joshua. He was promoted to leader of Israel after Moses died and was privileged to escort the people into the Promised Land after forty years of wandering. In a sense, he was their savior, offering them the peace for which they had been searching.

When you hear the term "salvation," what comes to your mind? If you have been around Christianity for any length of time, the word likely triggers the idea of putting trust in Jesus Christ and assuring yourself of a reservation in Heaven. However, if you had never been in a church, you might understand the word differently. Rather than thinking about the salvation that allows one to enter Heaven, you might think of it as being rescued from a dangerous situation. That, by the way, is exactly what the word means. We must guard against allowing our religious terminology to cloud the meaning behind the words we use. The word "salvation" is not limited to the salvation of a soul. It simply refers to the act of rescuing or delivering someone or something that is in trouble.

When I was in college, I had the privilege of having one of my sisters there at the same time. While many guys may not have been too keen with this arrangement, it came in handy quite often. From time to time she noticed that I was helplessly trapped in a one-sided conversation with an adoring female in whom I had no interest. Beckoning to me from a distance, she provided the necessary excuse to extricate myself from my misery and bolt across campus to ascertain what my dear sister could so desperately need. We both knew that she was merely saving me from my distress, and I appreciated it greatly. We always appreciate being liberated from a miserable situation.

Fortunately, most of the situations from which we need to be rescued are trivial. Those of us who live in a nation such as the United States, where liberty is proclaimed across the land, do not usually think of ourselves as being in bondage. Our forefathers took care of that in the Revolution. However, just because we enjoy relative freedom from tyrants does not mean that we are entirely free. Jesus made this quite clear in a discussion with the Jews of His day who also thought they were free. He let them know that they were enslaved to something much more treacherous than political bondage. They were enslaved to sin.

Salvation from Bondage to Sin

In a conversation with some Jews who had listened to and believed His words, Jesus instructed them that if they would continue to listen to His words, they would know the truth, which would make them free. They found this statement rather confusing, as they did not consider themselves to be in bondage (apparently neglecting the fact that they were under oppression by the Romans). When they claimed that they were already free, Jesus pointed out that "whoever commits sin is a slave of sin" (John 8:34). Jesus was not referring to political oppression. There is a bondage that is far more disastrous than subjection to another man. Of infinitely greater peril is subjection to sin. Unfortunately, that became the natural state of man after the fall of Adam and Eve.

Have you ever noticed that in all the news reports we hear, the good reports really catch our attention? We find ourselves pleasantly surprised, if not shocked, when something positive is reported on the evening news. It has become abnormal. Why is that? The reason is that man is in bondage to the cycle of sin. He cannot get out of it on his own.

Man is full of selfishness and hate. That's why the evening newscasts are crammed with accounts of drive-by shootings, terrorists blowing up innocent bystanders, and nations fighting against other nations like a bunch of overgrown juveniles on a global playground. It's a vicious cycle. The flesh is insatiable. The more we sin, the more we want. We keep going back for more.

Can this vicious cycle be broken? It can, through the truth of

Jesus. Paul clearly pointed this out in his letter to the Christians in Rome when he stated that "our old man was crucified with Him, that the body of sin might be done away with, that we should no longer be slaves of sin" (Romans 6:6). If you have put your faith in Jesus, you have been crucified with Him. You have become a new person. No longer are you forced to serve sin. The power of the Holy Spirit gives you the ability to subdue your natural desires and do what is right.

The possibility of being rescued, or saved, from the power of sin is quite incredible in itself. However, this also ultimately leads to salvation from the eventual result of sin, which is Hell.

Salvation from Hell

The Bible clearly informs us of a place where the souls of those who are not believers in Jesus will be punished for all of eternity. This indescribably dreadful place is commonly known as "Hell." Although many people today think of Hell as simply a state of mind or a total fabrication, the Bible indicates that it is a real place. The most descriptive account in the Bible about Hell is found in the story Jesus told of a pauper named Lazarus and an anonymous rich man. While on earth, the wealthy man possessed everything that one could want. Lazarus, on the other hand, longed for even the crumbs that fell off the rich man's table as he gorged himself on delicacies. Eventually both of the men died, and Lazarus went to a place where he received comfort, while the rich man went to Hell.

And being in torments in Hades, he lifted up his eyes and saw Abraham afar off, and Lazarus in his bosom. Then he cried and said, "Father Abraham, have mercy on me, and send Lazarus that he may dip the tip of his finger in water and cool my tongue; for I am tormented in this flame."

(Luke 16:23-24)

The social standing of these men is not the focus of the story so much as is the distinction between their destinations. In Hades (one of the Greek words translated into English as "Hell") the rich man suffered excruciating agony. The anguish of Hell is multiplied by the realization that there is no way of escape.

Some people believe in the existence of a temporary Hell called Purgatory. Between death and entrance into Heaven, a person suffers through a "cleansing process" that removes "unresolved guilt."[2] Is it true, though, that after death we can expect to carry with us some kind of debt that we need to finish paying off? Is this really what the Bible teaches?

What these theologians miss is an understanding of the sufficiency of the blood of Jesus Christ for salvation. Paul wrote that we are "justified by His blood" (Romans 5:9). To be justified is to be looked upon as innocent. If we are rendered innocent in the eyes of God through the blood of Jesus, what debt remains for us to pay?

Worship God for His Salvation

God did not simply reveal Himself through His names and then leave us guessing if He was telling the truth or not. He *proved* His character through the death of Jesus and offered us salvation from both the bondage to sin and the result of it. The torment of Hell therefore needs never to be experienced. In His love, He gave Jesus as the sacrifice that would appease His wrath for our sin, that "whoever believes in Him should not perish but have everlasting life" (John 3:16). Speaking of Jesus, Peter proclaimed that "there is no other name under heaven given among men by which we must be saved" (Acts 4:12).

We can be well versed in all of the names of God that we have studied, but in the end there is only one that determines our eternal destination. It is the name of Jesus, which provides the only means of escape from Hell.

. . . at the name of Jesus every knee should bow, of those in heaven, and of those on earth, and of those under the earth, and that every tongue should confess that Jesus Christ is Lord, to the glory of God the Father.

(Philippians 2:10-11)

Reflections on Chapter 13:

The *Salvation* of His Name

1. How did God prove His love for mankind?

2. What does the word "salvation" mean?

3. How is a man in bondage even though he may live in a free country?

4. Does the Bible really teach about a literal place of punishment called Hell?

5. Of all the names of God, which is the most important and why?

6. Have you experienced the salvation that comes through the name of Jesus?

Notes

Chapter 1 – The Worthiness of His Name

1. James Strong, *Strong's Exhaustive Concordance of the Bible*, s.v. "1126 *benonee*," (Nashville: Word Bible Publishers, 1986).
2. Ibid., "1144 *benyawmene*".
3. Donald S. Whitney, *Spiritual Disciplines for the Christian Life*, (Colorado Springs: Navpress, 1991, reprint: 1994), 90-91.
4. Bill Thrasher, *Living the Life God has Planned: A Guide to Knowing God's Will*, (Chicago: Moody Press, 2001), 90.
5. Tracey Rich, "The Name of G-d," *Judaism 101*, accessed April 15, 2015, http://www.jewfaq.org/name.htm.
6. Mordechai Friedman, "The Sanctity of God's Name, Part 1: Erasing Sacred Texts from a Computer Screen," *Virtual Beit Midrash*, accessed April 15, 2015, http://vbm-torah.org/archive/halak58/21shemha.doc.
7. James Strong, *Concordance*, s.v. "7812 *shawkhaw*."
8. Ibid., "4352 *proskooneho*."

Chapter 2 – Respect for His Name

1. James Strong, Concordance, s.v. "5375 nawsaw."
2. Ibid., "7723 *shawv*."

Chapter 3 – The Importance of His Name

1. James Strong, Concordance, s.v. "1961 hayah."

Chapter 4 – The Power of His Name

1. James Strong, Concordance, s.v. "7706 shadday."

Chapter 5 – The Presence of His Name

1. James Strong, Concordance, s.v. "884 Beer-Sheba."
2. Ibid., "5769 *olam*."
3. Ibid., "8033 *shawm*."

Chapter 6 – The Provision of His Name

1. James Strong, Concordance, sv. "3458 Ishmael."

2. Ibid., "883 *Beerlahairoi*."
3. A.T. Pierson, *George Müller of Bristol: His Life of Prayer and Faith*, (Grand Rapids: Kregel Publications, 1999), 174.
4. Robert J. Morgan, *Then Sings My Soul: 150 of the World's Greatest Hymn Stories*, (Nashville, TN: Thomas Nelson, 2003), 15.
5. James Strong, *Concordance*, s.v. "5251 *nace*."

Chapter 8 – The Healing of His Name
1. James Strong, Concordance, s.v. "7495 rapha."

Chapter 9 – The Purity of His Name
1. James Strong, Concordance, s.v. 6664, tsedeq."

Chapter 10 – The Discipline of His Name
1. James Strong, Concordance, s.v. "1578 gemulah."

Chapter 11 – The Care of His Name
1. Phillip Keller, A Shepherd Looks at Psalm 23, (Grand Rapids: Zondervan, 1970), 92-103.
2. Ibid.

Chapter 12 – the Peace of His Name
1. James Strong, Concordance, s.v. "7965 shalom."

Chapter 13 – the Salvation of His Name
1. James Strong, Concordance, s.v. "5547 Christos."
2. Zachary Hayes, "The Purgatorial View," in *Four Views on Hell*, ed. William Crockett (Grand Rapids: Zondervan, 1996), 99.

Appendix A

OVERVIEW OF THE NAMES OF GOD

HE IS WORTHY

Elohim – He is Supreme
Yahweh – He Exists
Adonai – He is Lord and Master

HE IS POWERFUL

El-Shaddai – The Almighty God
El-Elyon – The Most High God

HE IS PRESENT

El-Olam – The Everlasting God
Jehovah-Shammah (A City) –The Lord is There

HE PROVIDES

El-Roi – The God Who Sees
Jehovah-Jireh (An Altar) – Jehovah Sees

HE IS SUPREME

Jehovah–Sabaoth – The Lord of Armies
El-Gibbor – The Mighty God
Jehovah-Nissi – The Lord our Banner

HE HEALS

Jehovah-Rapha – The God who Heals

HE IS PURE

Jehovah-Tsidkenu – The Lord our Righteousness
Jehovah-Maccaddeshem – The Lord our Sanctifier

HE DISCIPLINES

Jehovah-Nakah – The Lord who Smites
Jehovah-El-Gemulah – The Lord God of Recompense

HE CARES

Jehovah-Ra'ah – The Lord our Shepherd

HE PROVIDES PEACE

Jehovah-Shalom (An Altar) – The Lord our Peace

HE PROVIDES SALVATION

Jesus – Jehovah is Salvation

Appendix B

Chapter 1: The Worthiness of His Name

1. For what purpose did God reveal His names to His people?

   His names revealed who He was. Instead of the need to explain why He was doing something, He would reveal one of His names. That name would describe His character.

   As we study the names of God, we should be prompted to worship Him not for the things He does, but for who He is—His character.

2. How did the Jews feel about the written name of God?

   The Jews so greatly respected the name of God that they often would not even write it out. They feared that it would be a great dishonor to God if a paper upon which His name was printed would be discarded. Even in English the name "God" often appears as "G-d" when penned by Jewish writers.

3. Why is it important to worship God for who He is rather than just for what He has done?

His greatness is not related solely to what He does. His embedded character is perfection and holiness. He would be worthy of worship even if He had never done anything on our behalf.

If we worship Him only for what He does, what will happen when we do not like what He is doing?

4. What does it mean to worship?

Worship is declaring the greatness of someone so others can see it. The word translated "worship" in the Old Testament means "to prostrate" or "do reverence." The New Testament word carries the idea of a dog who faithfully adores his master knowing that it is through his master that his needs are supplied.

5. What are some ways you have observed that the name of God is disrespected in our society today?

Here are some possibilities:

- God's name is often used as an irreverent expression
- He is given lip-service but is not obeyed
- He is praised only when He does what we like
- He is ignored when His work is not understood

6. How can you show respect to the name of God?

Here are some possibilities:

- I can praise His name even when I don't understand Him
- I can declare His greatness with my mouth
- I can declare His greatness with my obedience

Chapter 2: Respect for His Name

1. What are some ways that our society shows disrespect for the name of God?

Our society uses God's name as an expletive to show strong emotion. Many people also flippantly say "I swear to God . . ." without any inclination of fulfilling the vow. We also give lipservice to God but do not honor Him with our actions.

2. What is the difference between taking God's name in vain and taking an oath in a courtroom?

Taking God's name in vain is using God's name in a flippant or uncaring manner. Taking an oath in the courtroom is permissible if one proceeds to tell the truth. Even God made oaths (such as to Abraham).

3. Is it possible to worship God in a church service that is not catering to our own musical preferences?

Yes. Unfortunately, we often worship our preference of music style instead of the God described within the lyrics. It is possible to worship our own traditions and preferences rather than God. Our attitudes during "worship" reveal who or what we are worshiping. How do we feel when a style is used that is not our favorite? If we feel animosity or self-righteousness, we can be sure our worship is misplaced.

If we find ourselves in a church service where our preferred music is not being used, we should ask whether the music in question is unarguably unbiblical. If not, we must understand that others may be able to worship God through this style although it is not our favorite.

4. How can we disrespect God through our prayers?

We disrespect God through our prayers when we pray without engaging our minds and hearts. Often we pray for no other reason than to impress those around us. Furthermore, when we attend "worship services," we may mention His name occasionally but that is all the honor He gets.

5. What does it mean to profane the name of God?

To "profane" means to "defile" something. Profaning the name of God means to disrespect it.

6. In what non-verbal ways do we profane the name of God?

Anything we do that brings disrespect to the name of God serves to profane it. As Christians, the world knows that we claim to serve God. When we live in sin we show that we really do not care about His rules. Furthermore, the punishment that He inflicts on us when we sin makes it look as though God cannot take care of us.

Chapter 3: The Importance of His Name

1. How does the universe point toward the existence of a supreme being and creator?

   The universe is incredibly complex, which requires at least some kind of intellectualism behind its origins. While this in itself does not prove the existence of God, it does show that the universe is not a product of random chance.

2. Discuss the implications of the name *Elohim*. What does it mean for us in our daily lives?

   Elohim, when used as a name of God, indicates that He is the supreme being and creator of the universe. The fact that He created everything and that nothing is a product of chance shows that life has purpose. This gives us the knowledge that our lives are not pointless. We were created on purpose and therefore there is meaning to our existence.

3. What is the significance of the plural word *Elohim* being used to refer to God?

   This shows a truth that would not be clearly understood for thousands of years—that God is a trinity. The Godhead is made up of the Father, the Son, and the Holy Spirit.

4. What is the significance of Moses introducing God to the Israelites as Jehovah?

   In the midst of their forced labor in Egypt, the Israelites would have been wondering if their God existed. How could He allow them to go on in their suffering without intervention?

God revealed to them His name "Jehovah," which indicates that He truly exists. Not only did He exist, but He knew about their suffering and would bring them relief.

5. What is the significance in our lives of God revealing Himself as Jehovah?

Sometimes we may feel that God does not exist. We may feel alone in our suffering and think that either He no longer cares or is only a product of our imaginations. However, He is the self-existent one who knows intimate details of our circumstances and will be there to help us when we need Him.

6. What does the name *Adonai* suggest to us about our relationship with God?

He is the lord of our lives, whether we like it or not. We do not *make* Him master; we simply *recognize* that He already is. Doing so will spare us the punishment we deserve when we disobey Him.

Chapter 4: The Power of His Name

1. How did Abraham show his lack of understanding of God's power through the births of Ishmael and Isaac?

When Abraham thought God took too long in fulfilling His promise to give Abraham a son, he took matters into his own hands by impregnating his servant, Hagar. He failed to understand that God works according to His own timetable and He can make the impossible come to pass.

2. Why should the fact that God is referred to as *El-Shaddai* prompt us to obey?

As the Almighty God, He has authority to demand obedience. Furthermore, as Almighty God, He has the ability to punish disobedience.

3. What is the significance of the repeated use of the word *shaddai* in the book of Job?

Job did not know why he was experiencing his trials. However, as we read his account we are privileged to be able to see it all from beginning to end, just as God did. It helps us to see both the reason for and the result of Job's suffering. Although Job felt that God had forsaken him, *El-Shaddai*, the Almighty God, was still in control.

We may often feel like Job, misunderstood by the world and alienated from God. However, we must realize that God is in control of our situation, just as He was in control of Job's.

4. What do we learn from the fact that Melchizedek is referred to as the priest of *El-Elyon*?

Melchizedek lived in a polytheistic (worshiping many gods) area and time period. However, he stood out from the crowd in that he was a priest not of any manmade god, but the Most High God. Because of this, Abraham gave him tithes.

We may be surrounded with many false gods (be they idols or intangible objects of worship), but the one real God is worthy of our respect. We may stand alone in our worship of Him, but God will bless our efforts, just as He did for Melchizedek.

Furthermore, Abraham recognized that the Most High God is deserving of our gifts. Rather than debating whether or not we should give money to God and how much we should give, we would do well to gain an understanding of who He is. If we do that, we will give out of our adoration of Him.

5. What difference did *Elyon* make in the life of David?

> David knew that the Most High deserved to be praised (Psalm 9:1-2).
>
> David knew that the Most High God had the power to rescue him out of times of trouble (Psalm 57:2).

6. What does the name *Elyon* teach us about those who seem to be getting away with their sin?

> They will not get away with their sin forever. Asaph (Psalm 73:11-13) noted that although it seems like the righteous experience difficulty while the sinners are blessed, God will eventually destroy the wicked. As the Most High God, He takes note of man's actions and will reward him accordingly.

7. How should the names *El-Shaddai* and *El-Elyon* affect our worship of God?

> When we understand the awesome power of the Most High God, we will come to Him with our needs. We will recognize our own incapabilities and show that He has power that we do not possess. Humbly approaching Him with recognition that we are powerless and He is mighty is an act of worship.

We also will worship God with our service, even when we do not see the short-term benefits of doing so.

Chapter 5: The Presence of His Name

1. How did Abraham deal with worshiping the one true God in a land where people worshiped many gods?

    He planted a tree or a collection of trees as a place that he could go to worship his God. Although all around him people were worshiping false gods, he set up his own private worshiping place.

2. How can you set up your own "grove" to facilitate worship to God?

    Find something that will prompt you to habitually worship God even when it is not popular among your peers. It may be a place in the woods or in your house. It may even be a certain time of the day that you set aside to pray.

3. How should the name *El-Olam* prompt us to worship God?

    If He is everlasting, then He is far greater than we are. He is unsurpassed in power. When we compare ourselves to Him, it is obvious that His superiority should cause us to desire to worship Him.

4. What are the positives and negatives about God's ability to see and know everything?

    He is able to see all of our needs. He knows when we are in trouble and can come to help us. Most importantly, He has the power to help in these times.

    On the other hand, He can see everything—even our sin. We cannot do anything that He does not see and we cannot hide anywhere that He does not exist.

5. What does God's future involvement with Israel teach us about how God cares for us?

    Although God would allow Israel to reap the consequences of her sin, He refuses to utterly forsake her. He will one day make Israel a great nation with Jerusalem as the capital.

    We may be like the Israelites and think that God has forgotten all about us and has no interest in our daily lives. However, God does not permanently abandon His people. He is always *El-Olam* (the everlasting God) who is always there (*Jehovah-Shammah*).

6. Why is faith necessary when considering the fact that God is always with us?

    We cannot see God, so if we relied on our physical eyes we would feel abandoned. However, He has promised to be with us until the end (Matthew 28:20). Because He is the everlasting God, we can rest assured that He is able to fulfill this promise.

Chapter 6: The Provision of His Name

1. How did Hagar move from simply hearing about God's existence to understanding that He was involved in her daily life?

> She had heard all about *Elohim* from Abraham, but as she was all alone and frightened in the wilderness, it seemed as though *Elohim* either did not exist or did not care for her. However, an angel appeared to her and told her that *Elohim* was watching over her and would give her a son. She then realized that *Elohim* was not merely a distant deity, but a God who is present with her, meeting her needs.

2. How might Hagar have responded to God if He had seen her plight and ignored it?

> She would have realized that although God was powerful enough to see her, He was unable or unwilling to help. He would have been to her an impersonal God rather than one who loves and cares.

3. How could Abraham be so sure that he and Isaac would both return from the mountain?

> God had previously promised Abraham that Isaac would have children. Abraham had enough faith in God to know that even if he did kill his son, God would have to raise him from the dead so he could be the fulfillment of the promise.

4. Why is it significant that Abraham found a ram to sacrifice instead of a lamb?

A lamb would have been hurt in the struggle to free itself from the thicket. The ram, however, was caught by its horns. It would then be unhurt and would make a suitable sacrifice for the God who requires perfection. God provided exactly what Abraham needed.

5. Although *Jehovah-Jireh* literally means "Jehovah sees," what does the name indicate about God?

God not only sees the needs of His people, but He also provides. He does not merely notice our needs and ignore them. He saw Hagar's needs and provided what she needed. He saw Abraham's needs and provided what he needed.

6. In what ways has God provided for needs in your life before you knew you had them?

This is a good time for reflection. How has God provided for you? As you consider what He has done, your faith in what He can do in the future will grow.

Chapter 7: The Supremacy of His Name

1. Why did Martin Luther view God as Lord Sabaoth?

When he was in trouble, he needed a God who could fight. He was engaged in a battle against the corrupt religion of the Roman Catholic Church and needed to see God in His role as an army commander.

2. How should the name *Jehovah-Sabaoth* bring us both fear and comfort?

> It should bring us fear because as the captain of the armies of the universe, He holds sovereign power over us. He can effectively punish our sin.
>
> On the other hand, if we are obedient, the presence of this all-powerful God should bring us comfort.
>
> Remember the illustration of the military. If we are guilty of terrorism and come face to face with the Marines, we would rightfully fear. However, if we are stranded in a flood and the National Guard shows up, we will welcome them. It all depends on whose side we have taken. If we are living in obedience to God, we have no reason to fear His presence.

3. What does the name *El-Gibbor* mean for the persecuted church and for you personally?

> God is not weak. He is *El-Gibbor*, the mighty God. This is a military term and shows us that although it may seem for a while that the forces of evil triumph, God will have the final word. The persecuted church can take comfort in this, knowing that they will be vindicated in the end.
>
> Even those of us who are not persecuted for our faith must endure challenges simply because of what we believe. In the midst of our difficulty, we can anticipate the future when the mighty God defeats His enemies.

4. What is the connection between *El-Gibbor* and Jesus Christ?

Isaiah 9:6, a passage referring to Jesus Christ, says that the Child that would be born will be called, among other things, "Mighty God" (*El-Gibbor*). While Jesus is the savior of the world, He will one day act in His capacity of the captain of the hosts of God and lead the armies of Heaven to victory over the Devil.

5. Why did Moses call his altar "The LORD our Banner?"

Moses realized that it was not any man that was responsible for victory over Israel's enemies. It was accomplished purely by the power of God.

6. How should knowledge of the supremacy of God affect your daily life?

His supremacy should cause us to recognize that He is the judge to whom we must submit. However, His power also makes it possible for us to have faith that He can answer our prayers.

Chapter 8: The Healing of His Name

1. What lesson was God teaching the Israelites when He healed the waters at Marah?

He is *Jehovah-Rapha*, the God who heals. He used the healing of the waters at Marah to show His power. The Israelites had recently witnessed the devastation that God brought on Egypt. He was declaring to them that if they would consistently obey Him, He has the power to protect them from similar disease and punishment.

2. King Asa sought for help from physicians. Does this mean that it is wrong to go to doctors for help? If so, why? If not, what was Asa's real mistake?

> It is not wrong to go to doctors for help. Doctors and scientists have studied the God-designed makeup of the human body and have found many ways to heal diseases. Asa's problem was not that he went to the physicians, but that he trusted in their knowledge rather than in God.

3. What is the point of James' reference to praying and healing in James 5:14-15?

> James is showing that God hears the prayers of faith in regards to healing. Furthermore, his reference to the prayer of faith being effective to "save" the sick refers to the fact that some sickness is a direct result of a specific sin. In this case, the one who requests prayer from the elders of the church is admitting his sinfulness. God sees his heart and hears the prayers of the elders and responds with both physical and spiritual deliverance. The sickness is healed and the sin is forgiven.

4. What can be learned from David's prayer to God in Psalm 6:2?

> No matter how difficult our experiences are, God can provide healing. David said his bones were "vexed," or greatly agitated. He was not struggling from a physical ailment but an emotional or spiritual one. He knew that God could give him the strength to persevere.

5. What personal benefit to do we receive from God's punishment?

While we do not enjoy punishment, it teaches us to obey God. When we learn to obey God, we are enabled to fulfill our purpose in life. He places rules on us to keep us from harming both ourselves and His glory. When we abide by these rules, we can have a fulfilled life. His punishment encourages us to obey.

6. What lessons can we learn from God's predicted punishment on both Egypt (as prophesied by Isaiah) and Israel (as prophesied by Hosea)?

Sometimes God has to strike (punish) us before we realize the extent of our sin. Only then can He "heal" us and allow us to be all that we can be with His power. If He allowed us to continue in our sin without retribution, He would never receive the glory that He deserves.

Chapter 9: The Purity of His Name

1. What is the significance of the name Jehovah-Tsidkenu for the Israelites?

God has scattered the Israelites because of their sin. However, He has promised to re-unite them and bring them back into their land, as we see taking place today. When the return is complete, they will understand that it was their sin that brought about the original destruction of their nation. They will realize that God has blessed them beyond what they deserve and accepted them in spite of their unrighteousness.

The name *Jehovah-Tsidkenu* means "The LORD our righteousness." He puts His righteousness on His people and that allows them to be accepted by Him.

2. Why does God require righteousness to be placed on those who would desire to enter His presence?

He is righteous and cannot allow anything that is not absolutely pure to come into His presence. Because of Adam's sin, we have become utterly contaminated and no amount of washing can make us clean. The only way we can be clean enough to be accepted by God is to exchange our sinfulness with His righteousness.

3. What is the process whereby we can get the righteousness of Jesus applied to us?

The righteousness of Jesus is applied to us through faith. No rules, tradition, or religion is sufficient. We are so completely contaminated by sin that nothing we can do can earn God's righteousness. Therefore, He gives it as a gift to those who believe.

4. How does the observance of the Sabbath day illustrate the idea of sanctification and purity?

The Israelites were to set apart the seventh day of the week as a special day. This would serve as a reminder to them that of all the nations in the world, God had chosen Israel to be His favorite. The Israelites were elected to share His glory and righteousness with the world and were therefore given the Law to show them how God wanted them to live.

5. We have been set apart by God to show His glory to the world. Can you think of ways in which you can fulfill this responsibility?

> We can attempt to live pure lives so others can see the righteousness and power of God through our lives. We can verbally share with others about His greatness and what He has done in us, through us, and for us.

6. What is the best way to show worship to God?

> The best way to show worship to God is to honor the sacrifice He made through Jesus Christ and accept His gift of salvation. When you do, He sets you apart for His service. Then you honor him by living as one that has received this privilege.

Chapter 10: The Discipline of His Name

1. Why would God allow and even orchestrate the captivity of His chosen people in Babylon?

> True love holds people responsible. God showed His love for His people by not allowing them to continue indefinitely in their sin. The punishment that He brought on them helped return them to the realization that their calling was to serve God.

2. How does punishment indicate love?

> True love wants what is best for the other person. It is never good to allow a person to persist in destructive behavior. For example, a loving parent will punish his children, not out of spite, but out of a desire to see his child mature.

3. What is the difference between discipline and chastisement?

> Discipline is overall training. It is not a negative, but a positive, because it facilitates the ability to carry out a task. Discipline is carried out through various avenues, including chastisement. Chastisement is the punishment that is deserved when the student (or child) refuses to listen and obey.

4. How do you explain the fact that God punished the Babylonians after He had used them to accomplish His will?

> We may be tempted to think that success is an indication of God's blessing. The Babylonians were wicked people, but God was allowing them to defeat His people. However, the Babylonians were merely serving as a temporary means of punishment for Judah. When God was finished, He punished them for their involvement.

5. Why does God not punish evil as quickly as we think He should? What does this mean personally for you?

> God is slow to anger. He does not punish in uncontrolled wrath. However, we can be assured that He will hold the wicked accountable for their actions.

6. What should be our response when our "enemies" fight against us?

> We should be patient, knowing that God is the one who will ultimately bring retribution on the wicked. We should be thankful that He is slow to anger and has not required us to receive the punishment that we deserve.

7. How should we balance the love of God with His hatred of sin?

We cannot discount either His love or His hatred of sin. His love requires that He does not overlook sin. If we were allowed to continue in our sin, it would be detrimental to us. On the other hand, He does not punish out of unrestrained anger or hatred. In love He punishes and disciplines in order to bring us back into line with our purpose, which is to honor and glorify Him.

Chapter 11: The Care of His Name

1. What did David mean when he said that God provides a table?

He was not referring to a physical table, but rather to the fact that God provides what His people need. Often He even makes the preparations long before we know that we will have the need.

2. Why is it significant that God provides us a table in the presence of our enemies?

God never promised that He would remove our enemies (or any other trial) from us. He does promise, however, that He will take care of us while surrounded by them.

3. How does God restore our soul? Have you ever come to a place where you needed this?

He restores our soul by bringing it back to its former condition. Someone we get "down" or depressed. He is able to lift our spirits and comfort us as we face the difficulties of life.

4. What roles do the rod and staff play in discipline and protection? How do they provide comfort to the sheep?

    The rod was a short stick used for protection. The shepherd could throw his rod at anything that posed a threat to the sheep, driving it away.

    The rod could also be used to discipline the sheep. If an adventurous sheep wandered away, the shepherd would throw the rod in its direction, scaring it back into the flock.

    The staff was also used for discipline. The shepherd could reach out with it and draw a wayward sheep back to where it should be.

    The rod and staff provided comfort to the sheep because although they did not always enjoy being forced to do something against their will, they were being kept safe. No harm would come when they were close to the shepherd.

5. How did Jesus prove His dedication as a Good Shepherd?

    A good shepherd will put his life in danger to keep his sheep safe. Jesus did just that. He did not back down when faced with death. He willingly offered his life so we could have life.

6. With God as our Shepherd, we "shall not want." What exactly does this mean, and how do we reconcile it with the fact that we do have unfulfilled desires?

    It means that our Shepherd will take care of all of our needs. We are not promised that we will never fail to receive something that we want, but that we will never be "in want."

He does not remove brown fields, empty wells, and dangerous enemies from our lives. Rather, He gives us what we need as we experience these difficulties.

Chapter 12: The Peace of His Name

1. Why did Gideon name his altar Jehovah-Shalom?

   Shalom means "peace." Gideon combined the name of Jehovah with *shalom* because although he was scared after hiding from the Midianites and facing an angel, God had given him peace.

   Furthermore, God would provide peace to the nation of Israel. Although the Midianites had the upper hand at the time, God would fight for His people and deliver them.

2. Is a feeling of peace a reliable indicator that we are doing what God wants us to do?

   No. Although God can and does provide peace to those who are doing His will, we can have false peace. Consider Jonah, who slept in a storm-tossed boat as he was running from God. Peace is important, but it must be coupled with observance of the explicit commands of God.

3. How did the peace Gideon felt influence his actions of obedience?

   God asked Gideon to do some amazing things. Immediately after his visit with the angel, he was instructed to cut down the altar of Baal and replace it with an altar for Jehovah. There was no way he could do this without the peace of knowing beyond a doubt that he was doing what God wanted him to do.

4. Why does man not have peace and how does it affect his actions?

Our sin destroys our peace with God. We are therefore unable to do what we were created to do, which is to bring God glory and have a relationship with Him. This frustration is often taken out on others, resulting in all types of crime and personal fighting.

5. How can peace be attained?

Peace with God can be attained through faith in Jesus Christ. There is no condemnation to those who are in Christ (Romans 8:1). That provides ultimate peace.

Chapter 13: The Salvation of His Name

1. How did God prove His love for mankind?

He proved His love not by simply telling us that He loves us but by giving His Son to die for our salvation. His actions prove the reality of His love.

2. What does the word "salvation" mean?

While we often think of "salvation" solely in terms of forgiveness of sin and trust in Christ, the word simply refers to being rescued from a dangerous or unwanted situation.

In Christian terminology, we use the word to describe how we have been pulled from bondage to sin and punishment in Hell.

3. How is a man in bondage even though he may live in a free country?

    Although a man may live in a free country, he may not be free. One who is in bondage to sin is in a bondage that is much greater than anything the political world has to offer. The flesh, with its desire to sin, is insatiable. Sin leads to more sin. A man cannot be truly free until he becomes liberated from this vicious cycle and set free from the power and penalty of his sin.

4. Does the Bible really teach about a literal place of punishment called Hell?

    Yes. A short description of the horrors of Hell is found in Luke 16. It is a place where the souls of those who have never accepted the forgiveness offered by Jesus Christ go when they die. It is permanent because no amount of suffering can pay the debt of sin we owe to God.

5. Of all the names of God, which is the most important and why?

    The most important name is the name of Jesus. It is through Jesus that our eternal destination has been changed. Every person will bow before Him and recognize that He is indeed the lord and master of all. He is the only way of salvation.

6. Have you experienced the salvation that comes through the name of Jesus?

    If not, make the decision to trust in Jesus Christ today. Every person will bow to Him eventually, so why not now? Admit your sin to Him and ask for forgiveness. He will rescue you from the punishment you deserve and give you a home in Heaven. He loves you enough that "He gave His only begotten Son, that whoever believes in Him should not perish but have everlasting life" (John 3:16).

If you have any questions about this, please do not hesitate to ask. I invite you to visit www.benhammond.org if you need help.